NEO-PAGAN
SACRED ART
AND ALTARS

NEO-PAGAN

SACRED ART AND ALTARS

Making Things Whole

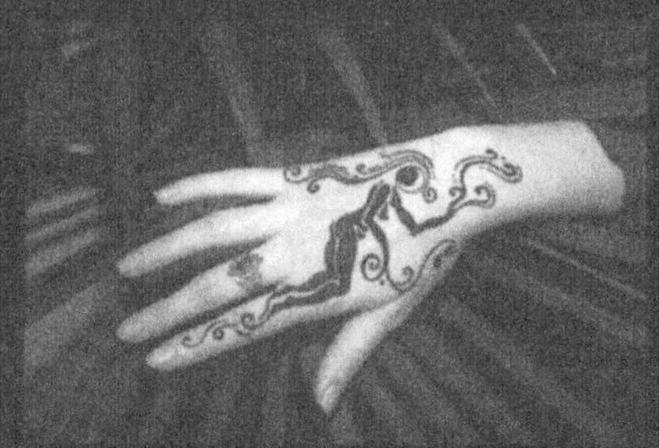

Sabina Magliocco

University Press of Mississippi
Jackson

Folk Art and Artists Series
Michael Owen Jones
General Editor

Books in this series focus on the work of informally
trained or self-taught artists rooted in regional, occupa-
tional, ethnic, racial, or gender-specific traditions. Authors
explore the influence of artists' experiences and aesthetic
values upon the art they create, the process of creation, and
the cultural traditions that served as inspiration or personal
resource. The wide range of art forms featured in this series
reveals the importance of aesthetic expression in our daily
lives and gives striking testimony to the richness and vital-
ity of art and tradition in the modern world.

All photographs are by the author.

www.upress.state.ms.us

Designed by Todd Lape

09 08 07 06 05 04 03 02 01   4 3 2 1
∞
Library of Congress Cataloging-in-Publication Data

Magliocco, Sabina, 1959–
    Neo-pagan sacred art and altars : making things
whole / Sabina Magliocco.
    p. cm. — (Folk art and artists series)
    Includes bibliographical references.
    ISBN 1-57806-390-6 (cloth : alk. paper) —
ISBN 1-57806-391-4 (pbk. : alk. paper)
    1. Neopaganism in art. 2. Decorative arts—United
States. 3. Folk art—United States. 4. Outsider art—
United States. I. Title. II. Series.

    NK1678.N45 M34 2001
    704.9'4899—dc21   2001022619

British Library Cataloging-in-Publication Data available

To my parents,
Bruno and Marisetta Magliocco,
who taught me to love art
by dragging me to every
major museum in Europe

contents

PREFACE

The first time I attended a large Neo-Pagan festival, it was an overwhelmingly hot, bright day—midwestern hot—and I had been driving for about an hour and a half out of Madison, Wisconsin, into the green and rolling countryside. Along the roadsides, the wild barley nodded its furry head next to blue chicory and yellow mustard flowers. As I drove my rattling old Rabbit down a steep gravel road into a large, oval valley, it seemed that I was entering another time or dimension. The valley was dotted with brightly colored tents, yurts, banners, and tarps, like a medieval market. People appeared in various stages of dress and undress, wearing everything from buckskin wraps and loincloths to long, flowing Indian skirts to elaborate medieval-looking costumes with intricate silver and amber jewelry. As I inched down the central aisle, where market tents had been set up for the selling of handmade jewelry, clothing, and ritual objects—everything festival goers needed to outfit themselves for the week-long celebration—a man passed my window wearing nothing but a peaked wizard's hat and what I then took to be earrings in his penis. I had already been doing fieldwork with local Pagans for sev-

eral years, but this was my first exposure to a festival atmosphere, with its suspension of everyday dress codes and the wide variety of groups from all over the country. I was so taken aback that I had an urge to turn the car around and head right back up that road to the highway. But the man must have sensed my discomfort, because he approached my window and said, "Hi, I'm Pete. Can I help you find something?" "Uh, the information tent?" I spluttered, not knowing where not to look. "Right over there." He pointed at an area to my right. "Thanks," I said, shifting into gear. "Blessed be," he said solemnly before wandering off.

To the outside observer, the material culture of the Neo-Pagan movement is one of its most striking features. The odd array of costumes and jewelry, often including the juxtaposition of neo-primitive and medieval-looking styles, can be off-putting, and contributes to the movement's undeserved reputation for attracting marginal eccentrics. Yet its sacred art is part of one of the most flourishing contemporary material culture traditions in the United States. There are Neo-Pagan blacksmiths, potters, tailors, silver- and goldsmiths, cutlers, leather workers, and wood carvers to rival those of traditional preindustrial communities. Nearly every Pagan ritual necessitates the creation of props, costumes, and altars that help participants get into the right frame of mind to understand the ritual's meaning. In fact, most Neo-Pagans are artists of some sort.

Surprisingly, the movement's material culture has received almost no attention from folklorists, and very little from other scholars of the movement, who have often focused on the social or psychological reasons that rational, well-educated, middle-class people would resort to rituals and the practice of magic (Luhrmann 1989; Pike 1996a; Carpenter 1996). My goal in this book is to call attention to that rich tradition in hopes of stimulating greater interest and understanding, as well as the undertaking of further, more detailed studies in the future. I am also arguing that the study of folk aesthetics can sometimes yield greater insight into the appeal of a particular culture and its politics than sociopsychological analyses: we may learn more about why people become Neo-Pagan by studying their artistic creations than we might by administering sociological surveys.

It would be impossible to cover all of the noteworthy art and material culture produced by individuals in the movement, and this book is not meant to be comprehensive or exhaustive. I have chosen to include a wide range of Pagan art, from simple homemade artifacts to the work of artists with years of professional training, to give readers a sense of the extent of the movement's material culture and the nature of its iconography. For most Pagans, it is the creative process itself which is the core of religious experience; it matters little whether the artist is a beginner or has a lifetime of experience.

I would like to express my thanks to the many people and organizations that made this work possible. I am grateful to Michael Owen Jones, who suggested I undertake such a study when I was a visiting professor in the Folklore and Mythology Program at UCLA during the fall of 1994. Part of the fieldwork was done with the support of a John Simon Guggenheim Memorial Fellowship for the 1996–97 academic year, during which time I was a visiting scholar with the Department of Anthropology at the University of California–Berkeley, where I was treated most generously. The New Faculty Development Grant I received from the School of Social and Behavioral Sciences at California State University–Northridge supported additional fieldwork and writing during the spring of 1998.

I owe my greatest debt to the many wonderful Pagan artists who told me their stories, shared their inspiration with me, and allowed me to photograph their work. Among them are Arios, Dennis Carpenter, Irish Clark-Savage, Catherine Farah, Selena Fox, Jana, Katya Madrid, Reva Myers, the members of the Bay Area NROOGD, Laurel Olsen, Karen Pearlman, Ellen Perlman, Raven, Lauren Raine, the members of Reclaiming, Rhiannon, Karen Tate, the members of Coven Ul, and Oberon and Morning Glory Zell. Gail Clark-Savage, "Lizard Frank" Cordeiro, and Judy M. provided support and encouragement when I did fieldwork in Lompoc, California. Thanks are also due to Thomas Albin and Kore for serving as models in photo shoots. Without the nourishing conversations and critiques provided by D. H. Frew, Anna Korn, M. Macha Nightmare, Holly Tannen, Tim Wallace, Sam Webster, and the members of Coven Trismegiston in Berkeley, California, this book would have been riddled with errors and inaccuracies, and would have been a lot less interesting. Finally, Steve Ho, Michael Owen Jones, Kerry Noonan, Susan E. Parker, Steven C. Wehmeyer, Izaly Zemtsovsky, and my parents read earlier drafts of this work. My heartfelt thanks to all of them for giving me a fresh perspective and many helpful suggestions.

ΠΕΟ-PAGAΠISΠ

AΠD SACRED ARt

Neo-Paganism[1] is an umbrella term for a variety of religions that draw inspiration from elements of pre-Christian polytheistic worship. The largest component of contemporary Paganism is revival Witchcraft, or Wicca. Within Witchcraft, there are many different sects, called "traditions"; some have ethnic flavors (e.g., British traditional Craft, Celtic Wicca, and *Stregheria*, or Italian-American Witchcraft), some are primarily feminist (e.g., Dianic Witchcraft) or political (e.g., Reclaiming Witchcraft), while still others grew up in a particular part of the country (e.g., Wisconsin's Circle, Massachusetts's Earth Spirit Community, and the San Francisco Bay Area's New Reformed Orthodox Order of the Golden Dawn, or NROOGD). There are also non-Wiccan Pagans who emulate a single ethnic tradition (for example, ancient Egyptian, Caananite, Greek, Roman, Norse, and Druidic practices) or who experiment with Afro-Caribbean and Native American spirituality. Pagans and Witches trace their heritage to a European magical tradition that they believe is a survival of pagan religions practiced by the ancestors of contemporary Europeans and Euro-Americans. Some Witches also believe that medieval witchcraft persecutions—"the burning times," as they are known within the move-

ment—were attempts to wipe out the last vestiges of pagan practice, and that medieval witches actually practiced a pagan religion whose roots date to Neolithic times. They see themselves as
the actual or spiritual descendants of medieval witches.

There is little historical evidence to support this idea. While
many pre-Christian elements did survive in European folk beliefs
and practices, they were not organized into a single, coherent religious system but incorporated into a body of folk Christianity.
However, revival Witchcraft did not magically spring into existence at the beginning of the twentieth century. It is the heir of a
Western magical tradition that dates back at least to the time of
the late Roman Empire and the practices of the Neoplatonists,
which were rediscovered in Europe during the Renaissance
(Baker 1996; Frew 1998; Orion 1995:79–103), when they assimi-
lated elements of Jewish magic and mysticism. Various syncretic
magical texts were preserved, along with charms and spells, in
sorcerers' "black books" well into the nineteenth century.

The contemporary explosion of revival Witchcraft onto the
cultural scene can be traced to the writings of British public
servant and amateur folklorist Gerald B. Gardner, who claimed
in his book *Witchcraft Today* (1954) that he had discovered one
of the last practicing covens of witches in England and that he
was initiated into their cult. While many scholars doubt the ve-
racity of Gardner's claims (Baker 1996; Kelly 1991; Rose 1962),[2]
his work became influential, and led to the diffusion of "Gardnerian" Wicca and the creation of similar traditions in Britain
and the United States (Adler 1986; Orion 1995; Valiente 1989).
The very words "witchcraft" and "paganism" conjure up frightening negative images for many mainstream Americans. The
fact that they are embraced by Neo-Pagans and Witches is a
clue to the oppositional nature of these movements: Pagans and
Wiccans construct their identity in contrast to that of the dominant American culture, especially a puritanical brand of Christianity that has historically considered the corporeal world and
its pleasures sinful and which reemerged as a powerful political
force in the United States during the 1980s. Part of the process
of identity creation involves embracing exactly those stereo-
types that are excluded from the dominant paradigm: in this

case, Romantic notions of the natural, the feminine, the primitive, the corporeal, and the wild. These qualities are recast as positive, a necessary corrective to the excesses of Calvinism, capitalism, and progressivism.

In the late 1960s, the feminist critique of the Judeo-Christian religious tradition became an important impetus for the popularization of Witchcraft as an oppositional discourse in American society. Many women who had felt excluded by mainstream faiths welcomed a religion in which the concept of deity included a goddess as well as a god, and where women had access to liturgical roles and religious authority (Carson 1992; Eller 1995; Spretnak 1994; Starhawk 1989). Feminists reclaimed the concept of the witch as a symbol of feminine power that stood in opposition to patriarchy. They looked to the past to find goddesses who could embody role models for women encompassing a wide range of attributes that went far beyond the usual qualities attributed to the Virgin Mary and the Catholic saints, or the strong women of biblical fame. Inspired by the theories of archeologist Marija Gimbutas (1994), many spiritual feminists posited the existence of a matriarchal golden age in which women and men lived in peaceful communities, agriculture and trade flourished, and all across Europe goddesses were worshipped as symbols of the earth's nurturing and productive powers (Eller, 1995:157–70). The presence of carved female figurines from the Paleolithic period was taken as evidence to support this vision. While the myth of a matriarchal golden age has now been critiqued within the movement, it remains a powerful sacred narrative that motivates many spiritual feminists to continue to seek inspiration from ancient religions and to work politically and spiritually to bring about a new moral order that includes feminism and environmentalism among its basic tenets.

Contemporary Paganism includes both mixed-gender Pagan and Witchcraft traditions and traditions practiced in women-only covens whose thealogy (a term they prefer to the male-centered "theology") focuses exclusively on a goddess. Many (but not all) mixed-gender traditions are feminist in intent, in that they consciously seek to oppose the oppression and marginalization of women in religion and society and to put forth new, egalitarian models for gender relations.[3] The feminine divine plays a central role in almost all Neo-Pagan traditions, and this is apparent in their sacred art.

At the beginning of the new millennium, Neo-Paganism is one of the fastest-growing religious movements in the United States. In 1979, Margot Adler reported estimating that there were about a hundred thousand Pagans and Witches in the United States (1986:3); in twenty years, the number has easily doubled. There are now over twenty thousand Pagan and Wiccan Web sites, more than a hundred periodicals, and dozens of annual festivals where Pagans and Witches gather to worship and create community. The majority of Neo-Pagans and revival Witches come to the religion as adults, through reading, political interests in feminism and environmentalism, and meeting with like-minded others, but there is a growing number of second-generation Pagans who have been raised in the religion by Pagan parents. Surveys have shown that most Pagans and Witches are better educated than the average citizen, although that does not always result in higher incomes (Eller 1995:21–23; Orion 1995:66–71). Generally, Pagans reject strictly materialistic values and choose occupations that allow them to serve others or to exercise their creativity and imagination. Many are employed in the fields of health care and computer science, while others support themselves by working as artists and artisans (Orion 1995:64).

Because Neo-Paganism is primarily an oppositional movement of the intellectual middle class, the highest concentrations of Witches and Neo-Pagans are found in urban areas and university towns. For the most part, Pagans and Witches live in ordinary neighborhoods; they do not set themselves apart from those with different religious practices. Some belong to covens, small groups of thirteen or fewer that meet to celebrate full moons and the eight sabbats (solstices, equinoxes, and the four cross-quarter days falling between solstices and equinoxes); others prefer to practice alone, perhaps coming together only at large public sabbats and festivals. In cities, occult bookstores may serve as meeting places for fellow Witches and Pagans, offering classes and workshops and sometimes coordinating large group rituals to celebrate the sabbats. National networking organizations such as Covenant of the Goddess also facilitate meetings and sponsor rituals and festivals, and allow Pagans to become involved in community service projects and interfaith dialogue with other religions.

The many sects or "traditions" of revival Witchcraft and Paganism differ from each other in practice, beliefs, liturgy, and style, though most share certain basic concerns and underlying principles. Pagans and Witches see the universe and everything in it as sacred, and divinity as immanent in the natural world. Their goal is to heal a universe they feel has been desacralized by the objectifying discourse of the Enlightenment and by the exploitation of natural resources and to return an awareness of the sacredness of all life to its original, central significance. By doing so, they hope to bring about a more meaningful moral order that includes respect for the earth, gender and racial equality, cultural diversity, and an alternative to conspicuous consumption. Inherent in these goals is a critique of positivist rationalism and its relegation of the magical, religious, and supernatural to a state of unreality. For Neo-Pagans, magic—often defined as the ability to change consciousness at will (Orion 1995:113–17)—is real, and they use it in ritual to heal the rift between humans, nature, and the divine. Ritual is the movement's primary form of worship and its most important art form (Adler 1986:252–53; Luhrmann 1989:230–31; Orion 1995:153–55; Magliocco 1996). The movement's main ethical principle is "An it harm none, do what thou wilt"—that is, do what you want as long as it does no harm to anyone; some would add "anything," including the environment, plants, animals, and oneself. A related principle, known in some traditions as the Threefold Law, is the idea that one's actions in the world are returned in kind three times over, the implication being that evil or irresponsible acts will ultimately bring the actor negative consequences, just as good acts eventually will have positive consequences.

While the movement constructs itself as oppositional to positivism and progressivism, Neo-Pagan goals are rooted in eighteenth-century Romanticism, with an idealization of the

natural world and of European peasants and the "noble sav-
age," as well as in nineteenth-century notions of cultural evolution. Many Pagans idealize ancient cultures and those of contemporary marginalized peoples, whom they presume possess a
spiritual relationship with the earth now lost to the dominant
culture. In an attempt to recapture this lost ethos, Pagans may
borrow elements from ancient cultures and from contemporary
indigenous peoples, producing the hodgepodge of buckskin
loincloths, Viking helmets, and flowing robes typical of Neo-
Pagan festival garb. This underlying aesthetic also explains the
appeal of things Celtic in the movement, as Celts have often
been considered the first victims of British colonial expansion,
the European equivalent of Native Americans (Chapman 1992;
Bowman 1996; Jones 1994). Pagan borrowings are not limited
to the past or to marginalized cultures; practitioners also draw
freely from popular culture (Magliocco 1996; Orion
1995:138–39). Rather than simply being emulations of a single
historical or cultural style, Pagan aesthetics are characterized by
a synthesis of styles from many different cultures, historical periods, and geographic areas and by the referentiality inherent in
the juxtaposition of these styles in a single piece of art. This
aesthetic typifies all art forms in the movement, from ritual to
music to material culture. Arjun Appadurai has characterized
this style as the "aesthetics of decontextualization"—objects are
removed from their original context and displayed as "tools and
artifacts of the 'other'" (1986:27–28). Their value lies precisely
in their ability to recall the authenticity and exoticism of the
Other, to induce a mood or style. But in many cases, Neo-Pagan aesthetics go beyond decontextualization, recombining old
elements with novel ones in ways that construct a new, syncretic set of references reflecting the poetics of the movement.

Neo-Paganism is often critical of consumer capitalism, especially in the sense that unbridled capitalism is blamed for the
devastation of the environment, the colonization of indigenous
peoples and the destruction of their cultures, and the alienation
created by repetitive industrial and service labor. Pagans are
not, however, opposed to any form of profit; as described
above, many sell their wares at festivals.[4] Their operations re-

main fairly small scale, though, and there is often a personal connection between the object's maker and its buyer. Pagans use what Michel de Certeau has called "tactics" as a form of resistance to create a satisfying alternative culture in which individual creativity is valued (1984). All forms of folklore are an important part of these tactics because of their emphasis on artistry, creativity, and small group interaction. The creation of beautiful and pleasing art objects becomes in this context a sacred act in and of itself. Several scholars have noted the importance of creativity in the movement and the imaginative and artistic nature of many Pagans (Adler 1986; Luhrmann 1989; Orion 1995:75, 121–22). Pagans value creativity highly. The central metaphor in many Wiccan rituals is the Great Rite, the symbolic union of male and female principles in nature in what many Witches interpret as being the fundamental creative act. Pagans feel that creativity is central to one's spiritual development and ability to contribute to society (Orion 1995:77). Because creativity and artistry involve transformation, these processes become analogous and equivalent to magical acts: the artist is by definition a magician (Orion 1995:56).

According to this paradigm, all art is sacred. But Pagan material culture tends to revolve around ritual, the movement's central type of worship and primary expressive form. Rituals are held to celebrate full moons and the eight sabbats; some covens also celebrate new moons, and spells, or "workings," can be done anytime. While in theory the practice of ritual magic requires only the will of the individual practitioner, in practice rituals generally involve at least an altar and certain basic tools. Large rituals can have many participants, and are much like theatrical performances, requiring costumes, props, lighting, and elaborate preparations. The Spiral Dance, San Francisco group Reclaiming's annual public Samhain (October 31) celebration, has over fifteen hundred participants and makes use of acrobats, dancers, a choir, and many costumes and tools, including four altars, one to each of the cardinal elements (air, fire, water, and earth), each created by a different Reclaiming coven. Pagan material culture tends to fall into certain broad generic categories: altars, magical tools, costumes, and jewelry.

ALTARS

Altars and shrines have been a part of the worship of many religions for thousands of years (Beezley 1997:91). They have traditionally served as sites of interaction between sacred and secular—a "place where humans and deities established, negotiated and maintained their relationships" (Beezley 1997:93). Neo-Pagan altars and shrines have their roots in these historical sites, in the magicians' altars of Renaissance occult practice, and in the home altars characteristic of vernacular Catholicism and other mainstream religions. Yet they also depart from these traditions in significant ways, forging their own unique path which embodies the poetics of this emergent movement.

In its most basic form, the Pagan altar is a place that holds sacred tools during a ritual. Most Pagans keep standing altars in their homes, where they perform rituals on a regular basis and engage in meditation and other forms of worship. Altars may also be constructed for a particular purpose: to honor a specific deity or to serve as a focal point for magical work towards a specific goal. Many Witches and Pagans feel that, in theory, the altar is optional; it is not *necessary* for either magic or worship, since the tools for that are internal rather than external. But it is helpful, because Pagans believe magic works best by stimulating and focusing intense emotion, then directing it towards the desired goal, a process they call "raising energy" (Bonewitz 1989:159) Symbols are important tools in that process; they are thought to communicate directly with the unconscious mind, which Pagans consider more powerful than the conscious mind. An altar is a place for the collection of those symbols.

Since Pagans believe deity is immanent, an altar can be made anywhere—on the ground in a natural place, at the base of a tree, even in an office or hotel room. But most altars are created for use in a circle, the sacred space Pagans create each time they do ritual. The altar can be located in the center of the circle, or in the north, east or west part of a circle or room, depending on the tradition of the practitioners. Followers of some Witchcraft traditions make altars in each of the four cardinal directions (north, east, south and west), instead of (or in addition to) using a main altar. The altar is an important focal point for energy. It holds ritual tools, such as salt, water, candles, and representations of deities; it can hold objects that evoke certain qualities for the practitioner; and it can be a place where the practitioner performs magic or acts of personal devotion. For example, to honor the beloved dead at Samhain, many Wiccans make altars with photographs of their dead relatives and friends, candles, and offerings that the dead might appreciate, such as flowers, food, and incense. They might spend a few minutes each day at the altar during the month of October, lighting candles and incense and meditating on their relationship with their beloved dead, or perhaps journeying in spirit to the Summerland (the Pagan otherworld) to commune with them. When I was looking for an academic position, my Wiccan informants suggested I make a jobs altar with a description of my ideal job, copies of my C.V., photographs of geographical areas where I might want to work, Tarot cards representing teaching and learning, symbols of universities where I might want to teach, and other objects that would help me focus on my goal. Of course, I was also researching available academic positions, applying for them, interviewing, and otherwise en-

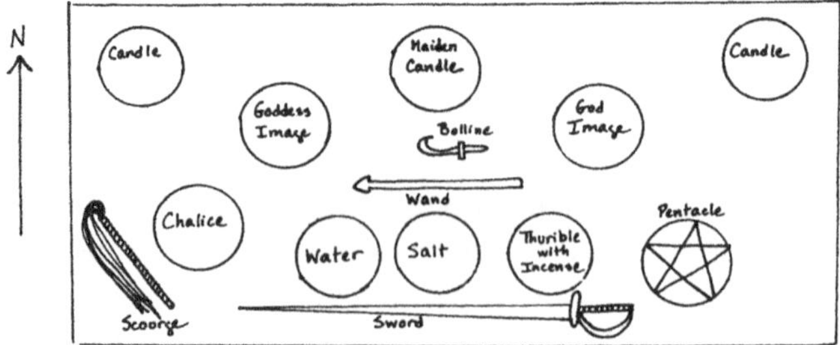

Figure 1. This composite represents the altars seen by the author at a number of Gardnerian rituals to which nonmember guests were invited. The maiden candle is the one from which the other candles are lit. The pentacle, representing the element earth, may also hold a plate of "cakes."

gaging in a job search; few Pagans would say that altars and magic spells alone are enough to obtain the desired objective. However, the altar was useful as a daily reminder of the focus of my goals; it helped me channel anxiety I otherwise would have felt worrying about the outcome of my efforts.

Altars are ephemeral art. They are often set up to be seen only for a few hours, the duration of a ritual, and then taken down. Although the individual items on the altar might be used again, they will be used in different combinations. Even permanent altars and shrines change constantly, as their makers' lives change and new items are added to symbolize new goals and objectives or to celebrate the seasons. Each altar, then, can be considered an individual performance—a display of the makers' skill and artistry, their grasp of magical symbolism and affiliation with a particular tradition.

Traditions differ from each other in the aesthetics of altar building. Gardnerians, Alexandrians, and other British traditionalists[5] use a single working altar, and tend to adhere to a formal altar plan with specific objects and designated placements for each object (fig. 1). These more orthodox practitioners believe that for magic to work, there must be a set of exact relationships and correspondences among magical tools, cardinal directions, and other elements, and that deviation from this pattern can interfere with the efficacy of the ritual.

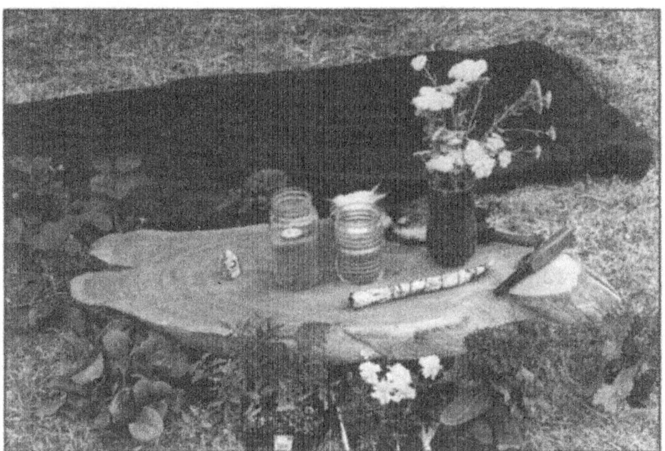

Figure 2. Simple altar for garden-blessing ritual, Lompoc, California, May 1995. The informal, relaxed style of this altar is typical of eclectic Witchcraft.

Feminist and other more eclectic traditions may follow a different set of aesthetics. Because they see deity immanent in every aspect of life, precise placement of objects is less important than the general intent of the ritual. A simple altar for a garden-planting ritual (fig. 2) features only water, salt, an incense bundle, a propane lighter, and a jar of flowers on a redwood slab, surrounded by the seedlings to be blessed. Reclaiming's ritual altars for each of the directions include collections of items suggestive of each element (plates 8–11; see figs. 5, 6). They are more improvisational, reflecting the belief that as long as the four elements and the deities are represented somehow, the actual form of the altar is less important than the feelings it conveys. These types of altars tend to be the most creative, since the altar's intent is essentially artistic: to stimulate an emotional reaction in the viewer. Altars are as often assembled by a group as by an individual; in these cases, they are examples of conscious communal creation, revealing the importance of community in this very individualistic subculture.

Whether formalist or eclectic, Wiccans and Pagans share a common set of altar tools and associations used in magical practice. These include objects to represent the four elements, such as salt, stones, and/or a pentacle (plate with a five-pointed star, or pentagram) representing the element earth and the direction north; a wand and incense, to represent the element air and the direction east[6]; candles and a blade (sword or athame) to represent the element fire and the direction south; a cup or bowl of water, and/or a chalice of juice or wine representing the element water and the direction west; and a representation of the goddess (and god—optional in some traditions).

Just as ritual is a liminal state that mediates between the ordinary, everyday world and the supernatural world (Turner 1968; Grimes 1990), altars can be seen as liminal spaces that serve as gateways or points of access to the world of the deities. The many symbols appearing on altars are cues that help Pagans transition from a state of ordinary consciousness to one of heightened concentration and detachment from everyday reality in which they experience contact with deities and personal transformations. Altars work through what James Fernandez has called an "argument of images" (1974:120) by stimulating the senses and emotions enough to "raise energy" for a particular purpose. As is typical in the Neo-Pagan aesthetic, images are often culled from different cultures and historical periods and are juxtaposed, creating both harmony and tension and inviting viewers to search for associations. With many images present, the audience can form a great number of associations and experience a high level of stimulation. In her work on women's altars from a variety of religious faiths, Kay Turner observes that these intuitively assembled collections of natural and crafted objects are at the very heart of women's spiritual experience, helping women to recenter the natural world and their connection to it in a world in which both nature and woman are considered separate and "Other" (1999:63). While this suggests that assemblage is uniquely a women's aesthetic style, it is the predominant aesthetic in both men's and women's altars in the Pagan movement. As Jean McMann's illustrated book on contemporary personal altars and shrines demonstrates, the process of assembling disparate objects connected by an idea seems to be fundamental to the process of altar creation, regardless of religious tradition (1998); the images accrue power through association with each other and with the altar itself.

Working Altars

Working altars are typically the site of everyday worship and magical "workings," or spells. Often dedicated to one or more beloved deities, they can be found in Pagan and Wiccan homes and at private rituals. A home altar to a beloved deity usually creates and maintains a reciprocal relationship between the devotee and the deity (cf. Brown 1990; Turner 1990). The devotee makes offerings to the deity, such as candles, incense, and flowers, which are thought to be particularly pleasing; in return, the deity helps the devotee achieve goals, solve problems, and feel a sense of protection. The altar is both the location and the expression of this reciprocal relationship. Working altars may have some stable features, such as images of the deities, candles, and magical tools, while other elements may change according to the seasons and the magical workings of the worshipper.

Catherine Farah, a southern California artist and member of the Fellowship of Isis, keeps an altar to the Egyptian cat goddess Bast in her bedroom (plate 1). In fact her entire home could be considered a shrine to the cat goddess: the walls are decorated with her own paintings of sacred cats, and in the yard is an outdoor shrine to Bast (fig. 3) and a toolshed the artist has converted into a Bast temple where she and other members of the fellowship hold rituals (plates 5, 6). Even her sheets and towels are printed with leopard-spot motifs. Catherine has been fascinated with cats ever since she first dreamed about them when she was only five or six years old: "Right from the beginning, my earliest memories, my earliest dreams always had cats. And [in the dreams], every night in our basement, I would go down, and there would be these wonderful large jaguars, and they were black with green rosettes on their

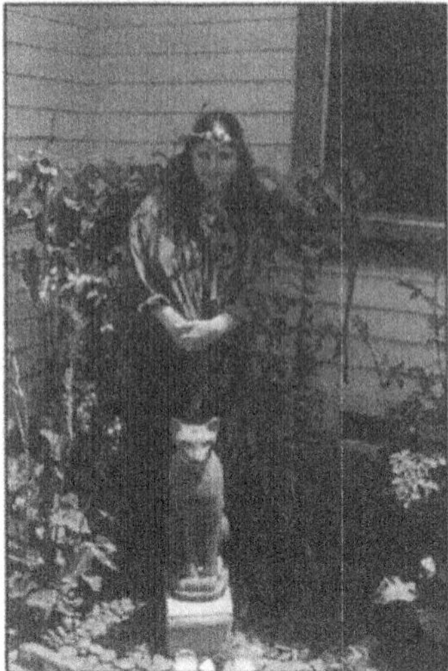

Figure 3. Catherine Farah in her outdoor shrine to Bast, made with commercially available garden statuary and stones. On her head and around her neck are ornaments with Bast heads, turquoise, and other semiprecious gemstones, which designate her as a priestess of Bast in the Fellowship of Isis.

fur, and they had green eyes with black irises, so it was like reversed on the eyes. And they were big—they were about the size of humans, only a little bigger, and they walked around on their hind feet. . . . They told me stories and they taught me things, and they were very friendly. And although they were quite ferocious looking, they weren't frightening. . . . To me they were real, or they still are real. I felt I was being prepared by these elder cats early on to live my life of devotion to the feline way."

Ever since, Catherine has devoted her life to drawing, painting, and sculpting cats. It was only later that she discovered, in the course of researching a history paper on cats, that there had once been a cat goddess in ancient Egypt. "I thought it was the most wonderful thing I had ever heard," she said. Still, many years passed before Catherine linked her interest in cats and Egypt with goddess worship and Neo-Pagan practice.

Her altar is situated on a low table in the bedroom, which she calls "my temple, more or less." On the altar are statues of Bast, the ancient Egyptian cat goddess of joy, fertility, and protection, and Horus, the Egyptian falcon-headed god. While these two deities were not linked in Egyptian mythology, Catherine has displayed them together here to symbolize the female and male principles in nature, a central metaphor for creativity. The crystal ball and pyramid reinforce this association; each is arranged before its corresponding deity. The altar also holds a crystal-tipped, double-headed wand Catherine made from driftwood. The wand is used for channeling and directing energy towards a specific goal. It is decorated with leather, fur bits, macaw feathers, and a tiny Bast statuette—all materials that have a special significance for Catherine—and is painted blue, a color she associates with Bast. The altar is also set with candles, flowers, and small stones and crystals, which Catherine calls "batteries," as they are believed to enhance the icons' power. Catherine uses this as her main altar, and may have several magical workings on it at any one time. The blue plastic Easter egg is one such working; it contains seeds, symbols of goals she had set for herself at the time of the spring equinox and which she hoped to accomplish by midsummer. Many components of the altar, such as the statuettes, remain constant, while others shift frequently, reflecting her changing artistic projects, goals, and desires.

A more elaborate working altar to Bast is located in the home of Catherine's friend Karen Tate (plate 2). At the center of this large altar is a smaller temple of Bast, which Catherine made as a showpiece for Los Angeles feminist group Circle of Aradia's 1998 *Circle of Altars* art exhibition. Done in an Egyptian style, it is made of painted cardboard and holds a fourteen-inch statue of Bast for which Catherine used stuffed cotton, polyresin clay, and fabric. The sides of the altar are painted with figures of Bast (left) and Sekhmet, the Egyptian lion-headed goddess bearing the sun disk on her head (right). This showpiece is displayed in Karen's home as part of a larger, more elaborate working altar to Bast and Sekhmet incorporating seven of Catherine's soft sculptures of feline goddesses, which Karen has arranged along with an incense burner and various other cat-related figurines. They watch over photographs of her own cats, Kitty (left; now deceased), Isis, and Xena (center). These remarkable pieces are reminiscent of the jaguars in Catherine's childhood dreams: they have cat faces and in some cases paws, yet they stand and sit upright as humans do. Their bodies are made of fabric, hand-stitched together and stuffed with polyester fiberfill. On these bodies, Catherine glues detailed faces made of polyresin clay with beads for eyes. The faces are individually sculpted and painted, so that each doll has a completely unique expression and personality. Catherine dresses them in costumes she hand-stitches from fabric scraps and decorates with beads and trim. On the left are the representations of Sekhmet (seated), "Felina," inspired by Lucy Lawless's character in the television show *Xena, Warrior Princess*, and Bast (plate 3). On the right are a seated figure of Bast, a cougar dressed as the figure "Strength" from the Motherpeace Tarot deck, with a Mayan cat figure on its breastplate, and another cougar dressed in animal skins and wearing turquoise jewelry (plate 4). The last two figures show the influence of Native American art on Catherine's work.

Catherine, who majored in anthropology and Native American studies at California State University–Fullerton, became interested in Native American cultures as a child because her great-grandmother was a Blackfoot Indian. While few, if any, Blackfoot traditions were preserved by her family, and Catherine does not consider herself a Native American artist, she became fascinated with this part of her heritage and began to explore it through reading and travel, eventually visiting a Blackfoot reservation to talk with local artists. She was particularly drawn to representations of wild cats in New World traditions: both the jaguar, sacred in Mayan and Aztec cultures, and the cougar, an important figure in the folklore of Indians of the Southwest. Her cat figures combine Native American and Egyptian elements: in their bearing and size, they recall Hopi kachinas, sacred representations of the gods, which Catherine collects, while many are modeled after Egyptian cat deities. Catherine's devotion to cats is evident both in her artistic work and in her dedication to political causes that help wild and domestic cats. She explains: "Whatever you do, in painting and art, to me it's a kind of sympathetic magic, whether you do it for that purpose or not. . . . [B]y painting things in a positive, loving way, you're bringing that vibe into existence. So I can bring beauty, love, the feline essence . . . into the world in a positive way. By people seeing them, it will . . . help raise consciousness . . . [about the plight of endangered cats] in this physical world. That's part of what my art's about."

Catherine's pièce de résistance is the Bast shrine, which she fashioned out of an old toolshed in her backyard. The six-foot-by-eight-foot room is painted a deep turquoise color and draped in leopard-spot fabric. Against the back wall is a low table with a box containing a large statue of the cat goddess, flanked by a row of reproductions of Egyptian Bast statuettes. The box, painted gold and decorated with hieroglyphic cartouches, or sacred signatures of the goddess, opens like a triptych to reveal the statue of Bast inside (plates 5, 6). This three-and-a-half-foot-tall statue is the largest Catherine has ever made, though in style and construction it resembles the artist's other figures. All of the clothing and jewelry are handmade, and the cape, headdress, and scepter are removable. The icon was the focus of devotions from Catherine and other women in the Los Angeles area Fellowship of Isis during an April 2000 ritual based on fragments of Egyptian ritual texts and hymns. During the ritual, Catherine dressed, decorated, and lovingly tended the icon as it received offerings from the women. While the beliefs and ideology are different, the practices of this group reminded me of the devotions to the Virgin Mary by religious sororities throughout the Catholic Mediterranean, who clean, sew clothing for, dress, and bejewel Marian icons in preparation for religious festivals. The icons are both mother and daughter to the worshippers: tended like dolls or small children, they are expected to reciprocate with tender care and special favors. In both cases, women feel a strong personal connection to the feminine divinity they venerate, who maintains an intimate involvement in the lives of her devotees.

It would be a mistake to look at Catherine's and Karen's practices and conclude that these women worship cat idols. What is revered is the presence of the sacred as it manifests in feline form. A shrine to sacred cats mystifies ordinary cats, elevating them to sacred status and creating a theoretical sacred "peerage" for them. These deified cats are brought into the home, domesticated, so to speak, and symbolically linked with household cats through their proximity. This exalted pantheon in turn looks after and protects one's household cats in a complex cycle of reciprocity. Like the cats in Catherine's childhood dreams, the sacred cats represent gentle, powerful parental figures that guide, teach, and protect devotees and their companion animals.

Community Altars

Communal altars and shrines, with their contributions of disparate objects from many different worshippers, typically embody eclectic styles. A classic example is the shrine to the Mother Goddess at Circle Sanctuary in Mt. Horeb, Wisconsin (fig. 4). Located on a natural ledge in a limestone ridge on the sanctuary, the shrine features female figurines from different cultures and historical periods: Neolithic carvings and cave paintings, a statuette of the Egyptian goddess Isis, a terra-cotta figurine of the Roman goddess Ceres, a bronze figure of the Hindu goddess Lakshmi, and many others. The juxtaposition of styles and images both invites viewers to see these goddesses as variants of a single mother goddess, eliding the differences among the widely divergent cultures that produced them, and allows the audience to perceive the contrasts between disparate cultural and historical representations of the divine feminine body. Another example is the community altar at Pagan Spirit Gathering 1993, a midwestern summer festival (plate 7). Individuals contributed to the formation of this altar throughout the week-long event, often bringing statuettes and natural objects from home. The resulting bricolage has an aesthetic appeal that unites the disparate images, which range from an inflatable globe (representing Mother Earth) to a deer skull (representing the horned god) to a Barbie doll in full ritual dress standing behind a tiny altar of her own, complete with magical tools. This ironic use of tactics involves an intentional reinterpretation of Barbie, a popular culture icon of femininity. The humor lies in the juxtaposition of two opposing concepts: the idealized but plastic im-

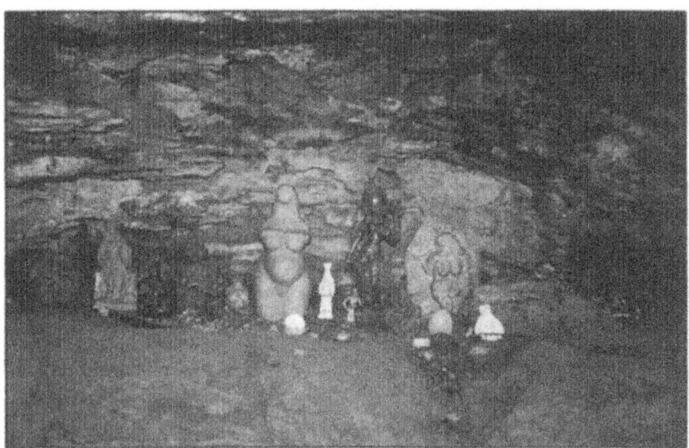

Figure 4. Mother Goddess shrine, Circle Sanctuary, Mt. Horeb, Wisconsin. Many different goddesses and female figures are represented here, including Ceres, the Roman goddess of harvest; the Egyptian goddess Isis; Lakshmi, the Hindu goddess of love, abundance, and good fortune; and several Paleolithic figures.

age of womanhood embodied by Barbie and that of woman as an earthy, powerful, alluring, and potentially dangerous Witch.

Each of these altars is a product of serendipitous communal creation, but a community can consciously work together to create an altar that communicates a message especially designed for a specific performance context. Altars encode messages that can be understood only by other Pagans who comprehend the complex system of correspondences related to sympathetic magic which underlies much of contemporary magical practice. For example, the altars made for the Spiral Dance by covens in the Reclaiming collective, a San Francisco–based tradition whose best-known member is the author Starhawk, each focus on a particular element: air, fire, water, or earth.[7] In Reclaiming's system of correspondences, air is associated with the intellect, knowledge, discernment, communication, the direction east, and the sword and athame, or ritual knife—tools that have the ability to cut, and thus to separate, to make boundaries, to create categories, much as the human mind does. The altar for the 1995 Spiral Dance featured chains of origami cranes fluttering from sheets suspended from the ceiling and billowing in the breeze of four concealed electric fans (plate 8). The audience members could feel air blowing on them as they passed by the altar, and could also see the many symbols of air (birds, feathers, ritual knives) before them. The air altar at the 1997 Spiral Dance inspired a very different feeling (plate 9). Here, amid blowing sheets and scarves in darker colors, a sword was suspended inside a hovering circular saw blade. This single, powerful image, completely in harmony with the element's correspondences, alluded to Reclaiming's chief political cause, the campaign to save the Headwaters Forest in northern California from the efforts of the logging industry. That year had seen the staging of bitter battles over the issue, including a demonstration during which police used cotton swabs to force pepper spray into the eyes of Reclaiming members and others who were demonstrating at the state capitol in Sacramento. The juxtaposition of images at the air altar encouraged the audience to consider various types of blades, their properties and uses: while an athame or a sword is used to create sacred space, the notched blade of a circular saw can destroy trees and entire ecosystems. Altars as performances acutely reflect the specific political context surrounding their construction.

Plates 10 and 11 and figures 5–7 illustrate further examples of assemblage in the elemental altars at Reclaiming's Spiral Dance. Plate 10 shows the fire altar from the 1995 Spiral Dance. Located to the south, the altar was draped in red cloth to resemble a flame into which audience members had to step in order to fully view the altar. Inside, the altar was decorated with foods and objects suggesting fire's qualities: warmth, passion, sensuality, courage, strength, and will. Included were hot peppers and popcorn (a food that explodes under fire), as well as drums, red candles, and sunflowers (plants that turn in the direction of the sun). Figures 5 and 6 show vignettes from the water altar at the 1997 Spiral Dance. Water is associated with the direction west, and with the unconscious, the otherworldly, the imagination, and the emotions. This altar was set up along a series of U-shaped tables. The tables were draped with blue cloths and deco-

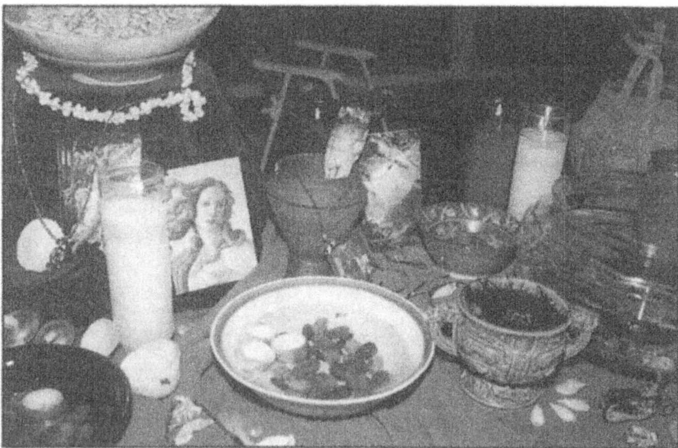

Figure 5. Water altar, detail, Spiral Dance, San Francisco, October 1997. This altar consisted of a series of vignettes arrayed along a curving set of tables draped in blue. Sandro Botticelli's Birth of Venus stands under a bowl of goldfish crackers in this vignette, juxtaposing high art and pop culture.

rated with a number of vignettes that featured watery themes: blue candles, seashells, pictures of the ocean, and pop culture items like rubber duck toys and goldfish crackers. Audience members were invited to participate by taking a stone from a container at the left of the table, imbuing it with their desires, and dropping in into one of the many water-filled bowls along the altar.

The Spiral Dance takes place at Samhain (October 31), when Neo-Pagans honor and remember their beloved dead by building altars to commemorate them (fig. 7). Dead ancestors and spiritual forebears are honored by the placing of offerings—candles, flowers, and incense—before their photographs. At the Spiral Dance, the dead are memorialized at the earth altar. The earth altar at the 1995 Spiral Dance (plate 11) was one of the most elaborate, with many vignettes featuring items associated with this element: dried flowers and seeds, rocks, gemstones, fossils, and photographs of the dead, whose bodies return to the earth to become part of the eternal cycle of life. Both Plate 11 and figure 7 show the strong influence of *El Día de los Muertos* altars on Reclaiming altars in California.[8] In this

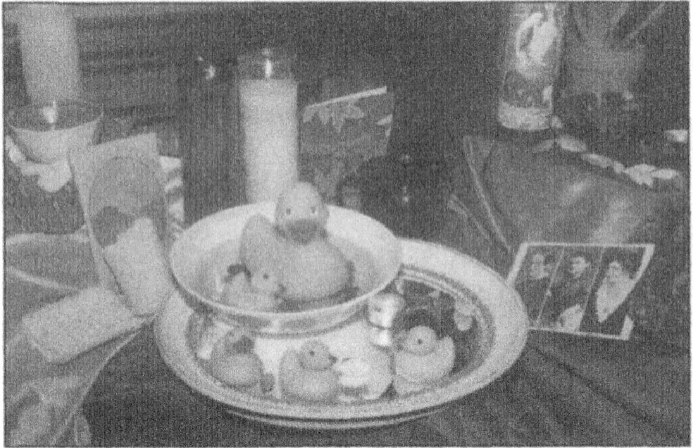

Figure 6. Water altar, detail, Spiral Dance, San Francisco, October 1997. Here, rubber duck bath toys are juxtaposed with photographs of dead ancestors. Water is associated with the direction west and with the Neo-Pagan otherworld, which is believed to lie across the sunless sea of tears.

case, Chicano traditions are being appropriated not for their exoticism, but through the process Robert Cantwell has called "ethnomimesis" (1993:5), the unconscious mimicry by which people take in customs, traditions, or culture. Because both customs are concerned with commemorating the dead, certain symbolism, such as the use of skeletons and photographs of ancestors, is easily transferable. For Reclaiming Witches of Mexican ancestry, this becomes an important way to maintain a connection to tradition while also adapting customs to a new set of beliefs and practices.[9]

Magical Tools

Magical tools include the objects and symbols that are found on altars and are used in raising and directing energy. Most Pagans and Craft practitioners share a common symbol set, outlined above, and a common set of tools. While not all tools will be found on all altars, most Pagans and Wiccans would be able to look at an altar in any tradition and understand the associations of some of the items present. According to the Gardner-

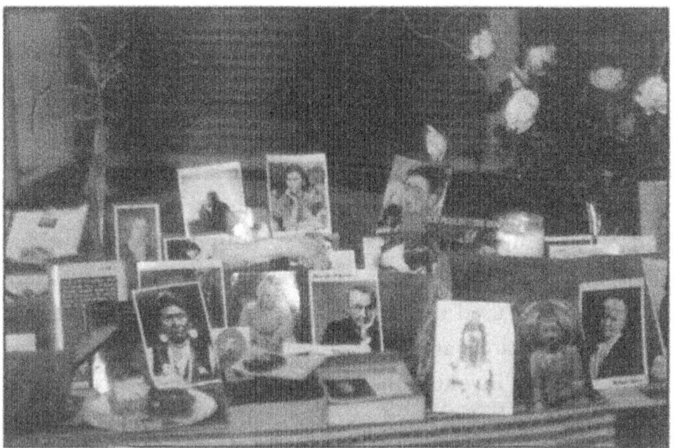

Figure 7. Earth altar, detail, the Mighty Dead, Spiral Dance, San Francisco, October 1995. The Mighty Dead include the souls of Neo-Pagans' spiritual forebears. Photographs here include those of Chief Sitting Bull, the Buddha, and artist Frieda Kalho.

ian Craft Laws, a set of principles found in most Gardnerian Books of Shadows, tools were originally supposed to be ordinary items, such as candles, cups, salt, and knives, which, because they were found around the house, would not arouse the suspicions of neighbors and inquisitors should the owners of such objects be arrested and questioned. If possible, Witches make their own ritual tools, because the creative act becomes another opportunity to imbue the tool with desired magical qualities. However, most Wiccans and Pagans make only a few of their tools themselves, and buy the rest from friends or vendors who specialize in producing them. Pagans may also convert ordinary commercial items into magical tools, subverting the item's original meaning and function, or layering new, esoteric meanings onto everyday objects. For example, several Pagans mentioned shopping at Pier 1 Imports, a popular chain store, for candleholders, incense burners, cups, bowls, salt dishes, and other paraphernalia. This chain's merchandise is often decorated with celestial motifs, which lend themselves to a Pagan interpretation. Many Pagans who appreciate objects with a history look for suitable ritual tools in antique shops.

One of the most important tools in the Witches' tool kit is

the athame, a ritual knife. The name probably comes from an Old French word, *attamé*, meaning "to cut" or "to pierce" (Baker 1996:177). It seems that Gerald Gardner (or the group from which he learned) was responsible for the introduction of this term into contemporary practice. The athame usually symbolizes the elements of fire or air, communication skills, mental and verbal acuity, the ability to draw boundaries and distinctions, and the power of fire to melt metal. In many Witchcraft traditions, it is used to cast the circle or to create sacred space by drawing a circle around the participants. The athame may also be used in invoking the elements. In some traditions, it is to be used solely for ritual purposes, and must never actually cut anything. Typically black-handled and double-bladed, it is thus distinguished from the white-handled bolline, which can be used for more practical purposes, such as cutting herbs. Skilled Pagan cutlers and swordsmiths frequent festivals and supply the community with handmade athames and swords. Athames and their sheaths are available in all sizes, from miniatures to long-bladed models. Athames can also be highly artistic and individualistic (fig. 8). This ceremonial bronze athame, from the collection of Ellen Perlman, was made to her specifications by a friend. Ellen chose bronze because of its warm quality and because of her fascination with Bronze Age artifacts, although the shape of the athame was modeled after the Indonesian *kris*, a type of ceremonial dagger. The blade is intricately engraved with labyrinthine curves, which Ellen feels give the knife a feeling of mystery and challenge. The handle is made of purple heart, chosen because of her attraction to the wood's unusual color. Ellen's athame is strictly ceremonial and cannot be used for cutting because of the softness of the bronze.

In feminist Dianic traditions, the broomstick or staff often substitutes for the athame. Dianics tend to perceive the blade as a symbol of male power and domination, and so may choose to substitute the broomstick, associated with women's domestic chores and witches' ability to fly. Ironically, in Gardnerian Craft the staff is often carved in the shape of a phallus, a sym-

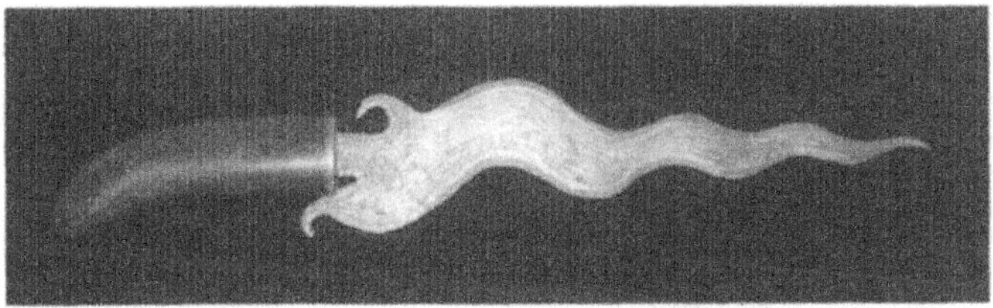

Figure 8. Athame, bronze and purple heart wood. From the collection of Ellen Perlman.

bol of the male deity's generative powers. Feminist traditions have chosen to reinterpret the staff in a vein more in keeping with their politics. There can be aesthetic reasons for choosing to cast a circle with a staff as well. Figure 9 shows a simple wooden staff carved in the shape of a goddess by Irish Clark-Savage, a Witch in an eclectic tradition. Irish explained that she has aesthetic, rather than political, reasons for preferring not to use a sword or athame to cast a circle: "I'm not partial to metal. For one thing, metal is cold. The only time I feel it's alive . . . is when it's molten . . . or when you're casting it, and then it's too hot to touch. . . . Wood has got a warm quality to it; metal does not. Swords are used for killing, but that's not my primary concern; I'm not that politically correct."

Irish carved the staff out of found wood as a gift for her partner, Gail. She prefers to use found wood for her carvings because she would rather not cut down a living tree: "There are lots of trees where Gail and I live; when the wind blows, there's lots of deadfall. Deadfall is nature's idea of what wood is. It's not manipulated, prefab, spit out like a toothpick. It has more of the essence of real wood to it." Because it was knocked down by the wind, she feels it is more "like an offering," a gift the goddess has given to her.

She carved the staff using only hand tools that she had fashioned herself—for example, a chisel made out of an old razor blade. The ethic of reusing and recycling objects appealed to her; in addition, she felt that because her power tools were so big she would not be able to carve the staff as she wanted, and "using hand tools allows you to put more of your energy into it." She chose the design because she felt "the wood had a

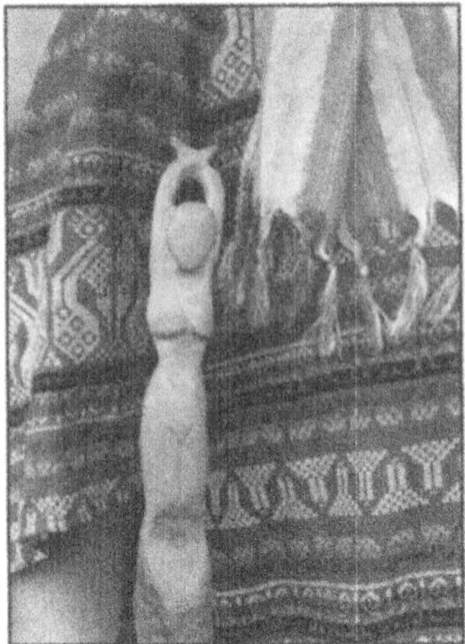

Figure 9. Staff with goddess figure, found wood, by Irish Clark-Savage. The goddess is shown holding a crescent moon in her upstretched arms.

graceful arc to it, it had the energy of that type of figure." Her preference is never to impose her will on the wood, but rather to let the wood itself suggest the form to her. Irish's comments reflect many aspects of the Pagan aesthetic: a preference for natural materials, respect for all life-forms, responsible use of resources and reuse of found materials, and a view of nature as being alive and imbued with sacredness, power, and artistic form.

Other handmade altar tools include chalices made from clay, glass, horn, and silver; bowls, dishes, and candleholders in various materials; and pentacles of etched copper or brass. Artist Reva Myers makes a complete miniature altar set in bronze consisting of athame, candlestick, chalice, pentacle, goddess statuette, and broom (fig. 10), which can also be worn as jewelry.

Representations of the Goddess and God

Among the most important items found on a Pagan altar are images of the deities. The representation of deities presents special problems for Pagans. Because practitioners of these religions often construct themselves in contrast to Christianity, they reject images of divinity associated with Christian, and especially Catholic, religious iconography, such as the static, beatific portrayals of the Virgin Mary and the saints. Instead, they seek new ways to imagine and portray female and male deities, often drawing inspiration from exactly those images

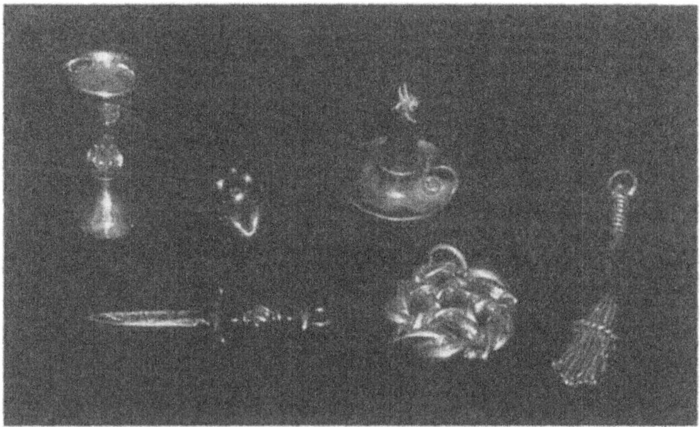

Figure 10. Miniature altar set cast in bronze, by Reva Myers. It includes (clockwise from left) a chalice, goddess figure, candleholder with tiny wax candle, broom, pentacle, and athame.

that represent the antithesis of Christian imagery. At times, such portrayals deliberately blur boundaries between nature and culture, human and animal, in ways that challenge everyday assumptions about the nature of reality.

For Witches and Pagans, the goddess is first and foremost identified with the earth. Like the earth itself, the goddess is changeless, yet ever changing; she is a nurturing force that supports all life on this planet, but she also has a darker face, for everything that lives must eventually die so that new life can be born from death and decay. These two contrasting phases of the goddess are sometimes called "the bright and dark mother" (Farrar and Farrar 1987:18). The goddess is also associated with the moon, and in this guise is thought of as having three aspects: the maiden, associated with beginnings, youth, and the new moon; the mother, connected with maturity, ripeness, and the full moon; and the crone, symbolizing old age, death, endings, the dark moon, and the promise of rebirth and regeneration. Besides this two- or threefold goddess, Neo-Pagans also recognize and depict many different historical goddesses as aspects of the divine mother.

Pagan representations of goddesses tend towards what Mary Russo has termed the "dis-ordered" or grotesque rather than the classical and composed (1986:213–15): that is, they have features such as abundant flesh, drooping breasts, and pregnant bellies (plates 12, 13), which are not usually a part of everyday representations of women in Western society. When these features do appear in mainstream depictions, they are usually meant to be either humorous or scary, as, for example, in representations associated with Carnival or Halloween. But in Pagan sacred art, these qualities are intended as neither. Instead, the artworks make a political statement about the nature of women's bodies and their relationship to the sacred. Breasts, hips, bellies, pregnancy, and fluids coming out of the body may be nonnormative for the *male* body, but they are part of women's everyday reality. By making images of the feminine divine that focus on and exaggerate these qualities, Pagan artists normalize and sacralize them; no longer grotesque, they become sacred. Janis L. Edwards argues that such artistic representations denote the "reclamation of the sacredness of female nature," an act she calls nothing short of "revolutionary" in a culture which privileges composed, classical, and slender images of femininity (1994:42). These figures, with their rounded breasts, bellies, and buttocks, emphasize women's reproductive and nurturing capacities and resacralize them by associating them with divinity. Many Neo-Pagan women whose bodies do not conform to the fashion industry's slim ideal identify strongly with these representations, which seem to literally embody the Wiccan expression of immanent divinity, "Thou art goddess." Some feminine figures sport animal heads, bat wings, tails, and other nonhuman appendages (plates 2, 3, 4, 6, 17, 18), visually breaking down the chain of being that separates humans and animals. But for Pagans, these images do not invoke horror or revulsion; they are seen as beautiful and imbued with sacredness, emphasizing the continuity between humans and animals. Pagans value these visual representations because they are thought to access the unconscious mind, which is believed to have a powerful influence on our perceptions of self and world. Hybrid images can change consciousness and alter our ordinary, rational perceptions of categories by speaking to our nonrational, unconscious selves. Through nonverbal forms such as dreams, visions, and artistic creation, the seeds of social transformation are planted.

The goddess is depicted as the earth mother or the moon; the god is more often connected with the sun and seasonal change. While the goddess remains constant, it is the god, her son and consort, who is born in midwinter, grows to maturity until the summer solstice, then slowly weakens and dies as the days grow shorter and colder. The god is often represented as the Green Man, a figure widespread in European folklore and usually associated with spring rituals and festivals (fig. 11). In this guise, he is generally thought to represent a vegetation deity. Like crops and other vegetation, he is born every spring, lives to bloom and fruit in the summer, and dies when he is cut down in the fall harvest. He spends winter underground, only to be born anew in the spring. A symbol of the cyclicity of life and the promise of rebirth, he is also seen by Neo-Pagans as an icon of environmentalism and the "greening of the earth" (Morning Glory Zell 1991).

But the Pagan god is also the god of wild animals, particularly herd animals, and of the hunt. He combines aspects of hunter and hunted, both protecting herd animals and culling them when it is their time to pass on. In this aspect, he is often depicted as a horned male figure, an image that is based on prehistoric gods of the hunt and historical horned gods such as the Greek Pan and the Gaulish Cernunnos (fig. 13, right). Pagans say that early Christians, in their zeal to convert country people to their new religion, interpreted these deities as demons, giving rise to Christian representations of the devil as horned and having cloven hoofs (fig. 12). Margaret Murray argued that medieval witches were in fact continuing the worship of a pagan horned god whom inquisitors mistook for the devil (1952:23–45), although the accuracy of this interpretation is questionable.

Pagans often turn to historical images of gods and goddesses for inspiration rather than inventing new ones. Generally, each tradition has certain primary gods and goddesses, often paired, who are considered tutelary deities: for example, those who embrace Egyptian traditions usually worship (among other deities) Isis and Osiris, while followers of Norse traditions may revere Freya and Odin and those of Celtic ones Brigid and Lugh. In addition, each coven will often add special goddesses and gods of its own to those of the tradition. In some traditions, all goddesses are interpreted as being versions of a single mother goddess with many faces and forms; different goddesses might be invoked for different rituals, depending on their qualities and associations. Individual Pagans may also be personally devoted to one or more deities. All of these factors determine what images the individual or coven use to represent the deities.

Oberon and Morning Glory Zell, founders of Church of All Worlds, make hand-cast sacred statuettes that are widely used as altar pieces by Pagans throughout the United States. Most are made of hydrostone, a mixture of gypsum and plaster of Paris cast in molds, then hand-finished and hand-painted with oxides or acrylic paints. The couple began their artistic work when Morning Glory was collecting goddess images from around the world and found that some of her favorites were not available. Oberon began to make them for her, first molding them out of clay, then eventually creating molds from the clay originals. Figures 11, 13, and 14 show some of the most popular items from their collection. Celtic deities Brigid and Cernunnos (see fig. 13) are sometimes worshipped as a pair by Neo-Pagans, but were not considered consorts in Celtic mythology.

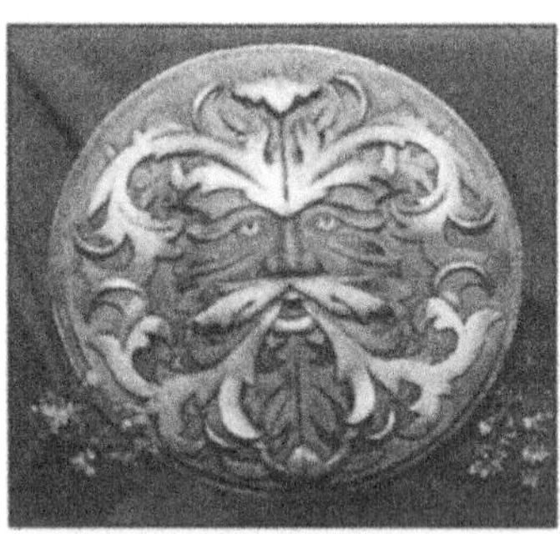

Figure 11. Green Man plaque, hydrostone painted with acrylics, by Oberon Zell.

Brigid is the Irish goddess of smithcraft, poetry, and healing; her worshippers once spanned northern Europe, and she was later Christianized as St. Brigit. She was connected with the hearth fire as well as with sacred wells and springs. Here, she

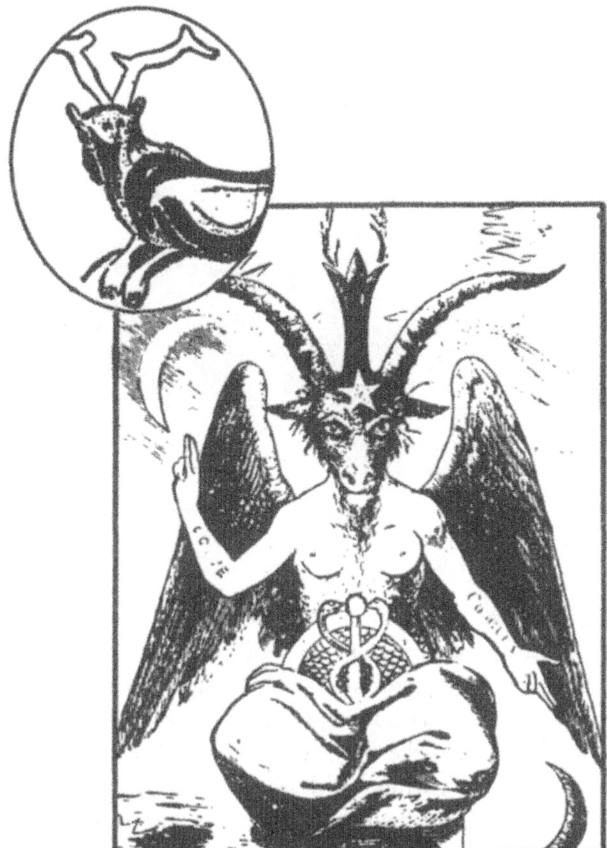

Figure 12. Early Christians may have misunderstood horned gods of the herd and hunt (upper left), believing them to be the devil.

carries a spear to protect hearth and home. This representation of Cernunnos, the horned god, is taken from the Gundestrup Cauldron, where he appears to be a protector and generator of animals. He is associated with successful hunting, abundance, fertility, and virility. Yet because hunting ends inevitably with death, he is also connected with the underworld.

Sekhmet (fig. 14; also depicted in plates 2, 3) was the lion-headed Egyptian goddess of the midday sun. She was a warrior goddess and, like the fierce lioness who defends her cubs, a

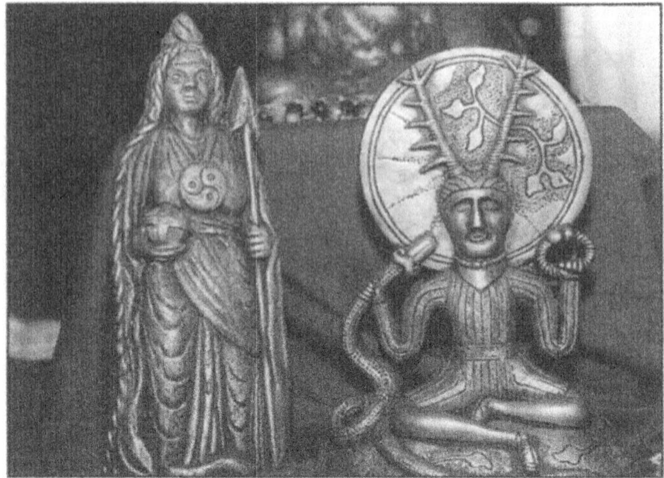

Figure 13. Brigid and Cernunnos sacred statuettes, hydrostone, by Morning Glory and Oberon Zell.

strong protector of her devotees, who included women, children, and the poor. She could also be bloodthirsty in her righteous anger, and was associated with drought. Here, Morning Glory has depicted her holding the ankh, a symbol of life, and bearing on her head the fiery sun disk, the "Eye of Ra," surrounded by a cobra, symbol of death and rebirth.

While many of the figures are inspired by historical artifacts, Oberon's Millennial Gaia (plate 12) represents a radical departure from the aesthetic of decontextualization: an attempt to create a new iconography incorporating Pagan politics and poetics. The polyresin statuette shows a pregnant goddess sitting cross-legged, her hands supporting her swollen belly, which is the planet earth. Her navel is positioned so that it is located at Delphi, the site of the ancient oracle and the *omphalos mundi* (navel of the world). Her left breast represents the moon, "whose phases beat the pulse of the ocean's tides and women's cycles" (Zell, Zell, and Gabriel 1998), while her right breast is covered with fruits and vegetables, the nourishing bounty of the earth. Etched along her legs are all manner of sea creatures representing "the evolution of life in the seas, from the earliest

bacteria and single-cell pro-
tozoa, to the great sea mam-
mals on her buttocks" (Zell,
Zell, and Gabriel 1998),
while her arms depict a similar pattern, culminating in
climax forests. Crawling in
her hair are creatures representing the evolution of life
on earth, beginning with
amphibians at the base of
her spine and culminating
in a human child over the
left (analytical) hemisphere
of her brain. Also in her hair
are insects and flowers, each
with its own symbolic associations: the scarab (Egypt),

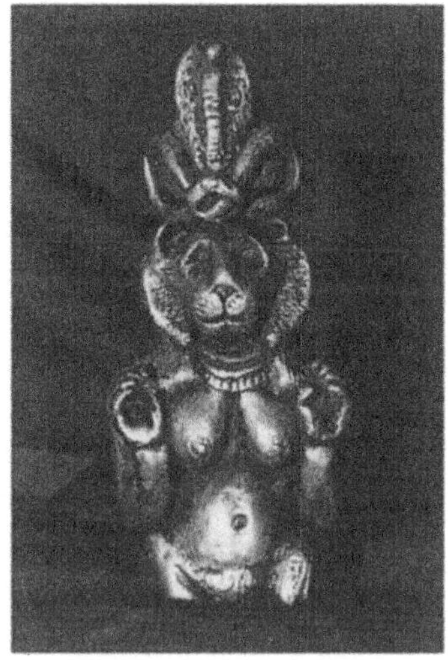

Figure 14. Sekhmet, hydrostone painted with chromium oxide and gold paint, by Morning Glory Zell.

spider (trickster and creator in African sacred narrative), monarch
butterfly (the sun), and luna moth (the moon). Within her tresses
is the double helix of DNA, forming the center of a tree of life
from which all the life-forms develop. Leaves around her face represent the fifteen sacred trees in the Celtic calendar, while her face
itself is designed to incorporate features from many racial and
ethnic groups (Zell, Zell, and Gabriel 1998:9).

Oberon Zell describes the experience that led to the development of this image: "On September 6, 1970, I had a dramatic mystical experience that altered dramatically the course
of my life and work. While a few hours went by on the clock, I
experienced through my own body the entire history and consciousness of the living Earth. It was an experience of going
back to the first cell that ever was and dividing until I felt my
own presence, through the DNA molecule, in all life and the
presence of all life inside me. Immense information and wisdom of Gaia flooded through me, and I felt irrevocably bonded
to Her and blessed by Her. Since then, Her living presence has
never left me" (1998:4–5).

After many years of sculpting sacred figurines, in 1995 Oberon decided the time had come to attempt to create a piece based on his vision of Gaia. "I wanted to craft a sculpture that any person on Earth could look at and feel something of what I experienced when She first touched my soul . . . a 'sermon in stone' that would convey the Gaia Thesis to anyone who beheld it" (1998:9). He began working on a sculpture, using friends and family as models. In order to see the intricate details of the creatures he was forming, he worked wearing magnifying glasses much of the time. He reports that, as he worked on the sculpture, "I felt my hands were no longer my own, and I found myself almost a fascinated observer as the figure of the Goddess began to form itself through my hands" (1998:9).

The Zells are among the few Pagan artisans who have actually taken their work into mass production. Some of the figures, including the Millennial Gaia, are produced overseas from Oberon's and Morning Glory's original designs, although most are hand-finished and painted in the Zells' small workshop in northern California. For Oberon, making such art remains a sacred calling, despite the fact that high demand for his pieces has pushed him into mechanizing certain aspects of production and employing a business manager. "As an artist, creating sacred art as a means of right livelihood is the highest calling. . . . To know the work you are doing helps people create their own connections with the sacred, . . . I really feel strongly about that."[10] When he visits Pagan homes and sees one of his and Morning Glory's statues on the altar, he says, "It's a wonderful feeling."[11]

COSTUME

A strange change comes over me when I go to a Pagan gathering, and it starts with clothing. I arrived at the Pantheacon Neo-Pagan conference wearing plain, warm, comfortable clothes, but almost as soon as I started unpacking in my hotel room, I began to look strange to myself. What was this white turtleneck? Why was I wearing a preppy sweater and hiking boots? I started changing various items of clothing, adding a black fleece cardigan and a witchy necklace, but they still looked wrong against the white turtleneck. I ended up changing completely: black dress, black tights, soft pointed suede shoes, an amber and garnet necklace and earrings, my grandmother's topaz ring, body glitter, and a black shawl printed wildly with suns and moons. In this outfit, which I would never wear in my academic life, but which is plain by Pagan standards, I finally felt comfortable enough to emerge from my room.

As I observed at the beginning of this book, Neo-Pagan costuming is one of its most distinctive features. Folk costume is a "visible, outward badge of folk-group identity, worn consciously to express that identity" (Yoder 1972:295). It includes not only clothing, but all body adornments, including jewelry, tattoos and body modifications. European ethnologist Peter Bogatyrev first identified costume as a sign with manifold functions: practical, aesthetic, ritual, and ideological (1971). Folk costume not only outwardly symbolizes one's identity as a member of a community, but also expresses the individuals' multiple relationships within that community (Yoder 1972:296). Sarah Pike observes that for Neo-Pagans, the adoption of a new religious faith necessitates the forging of new identities; costuming and body adornment are ways in which to fashion such identities, especially in the context of Neo-Pagan festivals (1996b:121). Pike argues that "costumes, nudity and adornment are part of a complex system of coding" through which Pagans shape boundaries within their communities and express conflicting ideologies (1996b:122, 131). Costumes identify Pagans as belonging to a religious community, especially at festivals, where they mark the boundary between the everyday world and the heightened reality of the festival environment, but they also differentiate practitioners from each other in terms of religious tradition, status in the hierarchy, and gender. In this section, I will examine various aspects of Neo-Pagan folk costuming as it relates to sacred art.

Jewelry

Jewelry is one of the most important communication strategies for contemporary Witches and Pagans. Just as a person wearing a Star of David or a cross indicates his or her religious affiliation to group members and outsiders, Pagans and Witches wear esoteric symbols that communicate aspects of their religion, tradition, and rank. Because they must often operate in secret to avoid discrimination, they use jewelry as a coded form of communication and self-presentation. Even in a nonreligious setting, those who know the code will be able to identify and understand the meaning of the symbols, and glean important information about the wearer.

The most common symbol of contemporary Witchcraft is

the pentagram, a five-pointed, linear star within a circle, worn with the point facing up (fig. 15). The pentagram is an ancient symbol found in a number of different cultures and historical periods, but its use as a symbol of Witchcraft is rather recent.[12] The followers of the Greek mathematician Pythagoras (586–506 B.C.E.) used the pentagram, or pentalpha, as they called it, to symbolize divine perfection because of its geometrical properties. This symbol may have reentered European tradition during the Renaissance, when geometric symbolism once again became

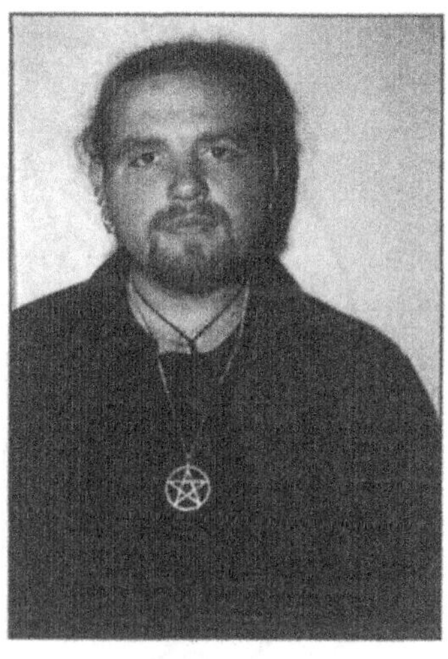

Figure 15. Thomas Albin, of coven Ul in San Francisco, wearing a classic silver pentagram and a holy stone amulet. Stones with natural holes in them have long been considered magical talismans in many parts of Europe and the United States.

important. Henry Cornelius Agrippa von Nettesheim, a sixteenth-century German magician and early scientist, drew an upright pentagram superimposed on the human body to show the perfection of the human form and its harmony with the four elements of matter (air, fire, water, and earth) and the planets (fig. 16). His contemporary, the Italian philosopher Giordano Bruno, reproduced a similar figure (fig. 17) symbolizing the centrality of the number five to the human soul. Perhaps because Bruno and other Renaissance philosophers and magicians were executed as heretics by the Inquisition, this symbol became associated with witchcraft and evil deeds. But the five-pointed star is also known in Jewish magical tradition as the Seal of Solomon, in contrast to the six-pointed Star of David. It may have become associated with witches during the medieval persecutions, as did other Jewish symbols such as the Sabbath and synagogue, in an attempt to slander them, or perhaps it entered modern

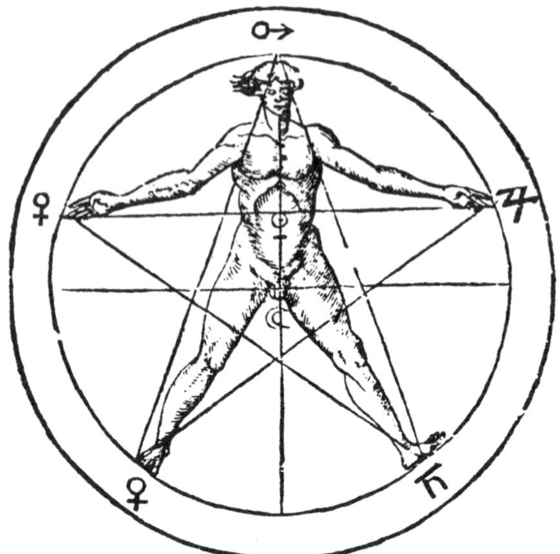

Figure 16. Human Form Divine, from Agrippa von Nettesheim's De occulta philosophia (1531).

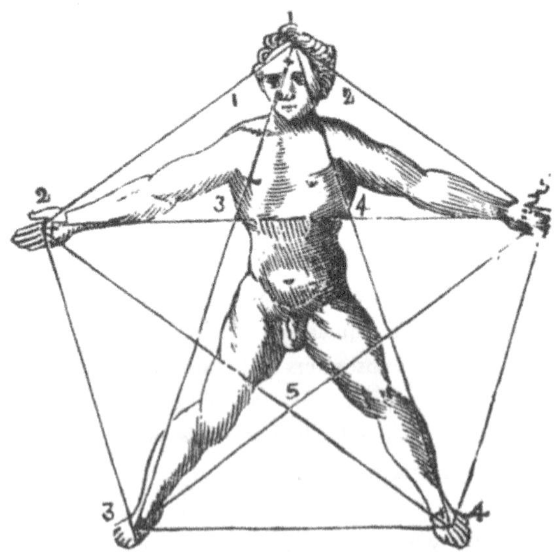

Figure 17. The image of good fortune, or Jupiter, from Giordano Bruno's About the Monas (1591).

occult tradition through the *Key of Solomon*, a set of Hebrew magical texts from the late Middle Ages. Its use as a symbol of contemporary Witchcraft probably began with Gerald Gardner's adaptation of it in the emblems for the second and third degrees of initiation in Gardnerian Craft, but since the 1960s it has spread to all the Wiccan-based traditions.

Most Wiccans and Pagans say the pentagram represents the four cardinal elements of matter, plus spirit. The spirit point appears at the top of the star, presiding over the others. In some traditions, each point is also associated with a specific quality: in the Reclaiming tradition, for example, love, wisdom, knowledge, law, and power are points in the "pentacle of pearl." The circle is associated with the cycle of life and with the magic circle, or sacred ritual space. Witches often wear a pentagram hanging on a chain or cord around their necks, as Thomas Albin does in figure 15. Pentagrams, like much Pagan jewelry, are often made of silver, both because of its association with the moon and the goddess Diana (and thus goddesses in general), and because it is relatively inexpensive compared to other precious metals. Other common symbols used in Pagan jewelry include ankhs, Thor's hammers, Celtic knotwork designs, animals, and female figures. Each of these communicates important aspects of the wearer's identity and affiliation. The ankh, an ancient Egyptian symbol of life, is often worn by members of the Fellowship of Isis and other Egyptian revival groups (fig. 18), while the hammer of Thor almost al-

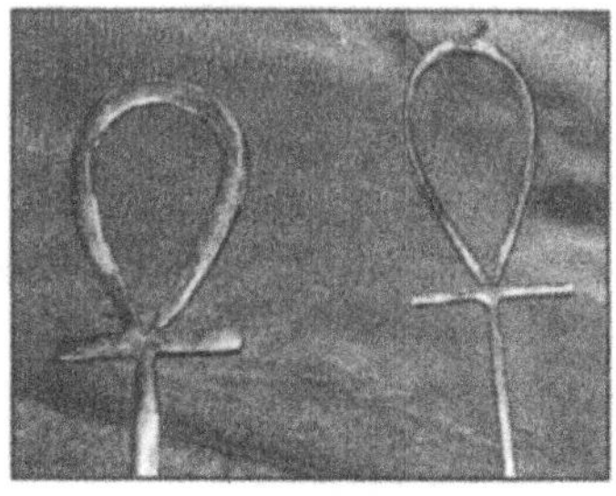

Figure 18. Ankh ornaments, bronze, by Harry Pearlman. The ankh is the ancient Egyptian symbol of life.

ways indicates that the wearer is a member of one of the Norse groups. Practitioners of "Celtic" Wicca often choose designs inspired by knotwork of medieval Irish stone carvings and manuscripts. Spiral motifs, symbolizing the never-ending cycle of life, are also popular. An animal pendant usually indicates that the creature has a special significance to the wearer. Many Pagans speak of certain animals as their "totems," borrowing the term from anthropological parlance. To Neo-Pagans, a totem animal is one which embodies certain qualities for which they feel an affinity. The concept has been syncretized with the European legend of the witches' familiar, an animal that assists the witch in her magical practice, so that the two terms are often taken as variants of the same concept. Although in theory any animal can be a totem, the most popular ones are associated with positive symbolic qualities that are valued by the dominant culture as well. Cats, wolves, and birds, especially eagles and ravens, are totems that turn up frequently in representations; they can symbolize qualities such as independence, strength, and courage. I have also seen more unusual totem animals, such as bats, bison, frogs, lemurs, lizards, and opossums; in these cases, the animals have unique personal associations for those who choose them as totems.[13]

Pagans may also wear jewelry as amulets or talismans (figs. 19–21). Jewelry can be imbued with magical energy and good wishes to bring the wearer good luck, strength, and other desired blessings according to the system of metaphors known as "magical correspondences." In this ancient system based on the principles of sympathetic magic, each deity is associated with certain planets, colors, minerals, plants, animals, and numbers; any of these may be used to represent that deity or the qualities associated with it. For example, Jupiter, bringer of good luck and prosperity in the ancient Roman pantheon, is associated with the planet Jupiter, the number eight, the colors purple and dark blue, the aspen tree, the horse, and the minerals gold and potassium. An amulet for good luck and prosperity might incorporate any or all of these symbols. Other symbols can also be combined in amulets and talismans. For example, a molecular biologist who was just becoming proficient in DNA sequencing purchased a fused glass amulet engraved with a rune meaning "skill." She liked the appearance of the piece, and felt it would help her concentrate on learning the necessary skills

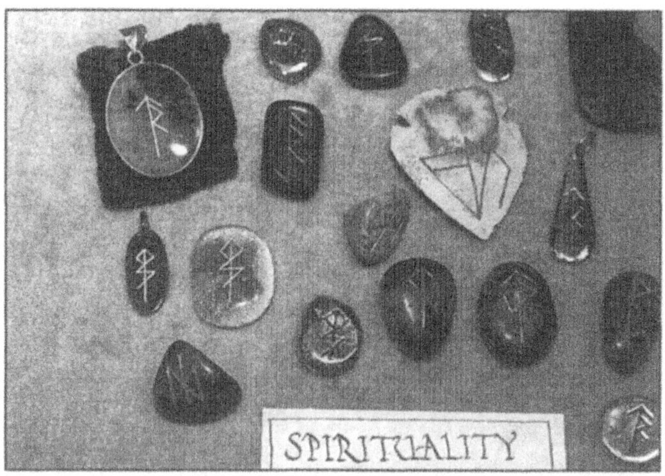

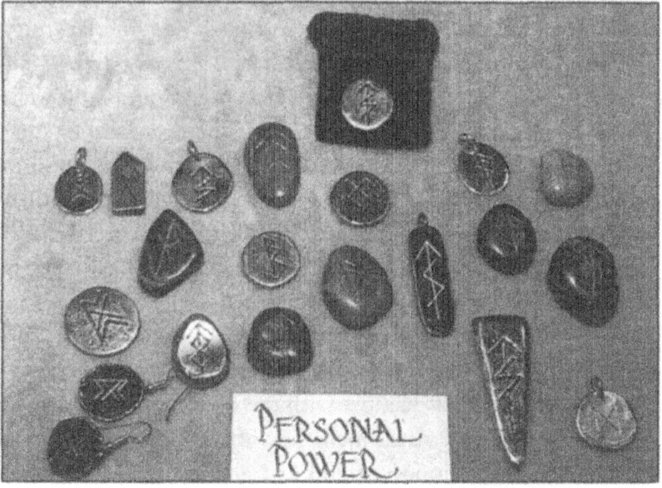

Figures 19 and 20. Amulets, fused glass and stone, by Nancy Pearlman and Karen Pearlman. The amulets are engraved with combinations of runes signifying the desired qualities, and can be worn as jewelry. The runic alphabet was used by peoples in northern Europe, and has now been revived and adapted for magical use. Each letter has a pictographic meaning, as well as a phonetic value.

she needed in her new job. Jewelry that is not specifically Pagan can be adapted to magical uses, too. A Wiccan elder about to engage in a debate made a talisman incorporating the qualities

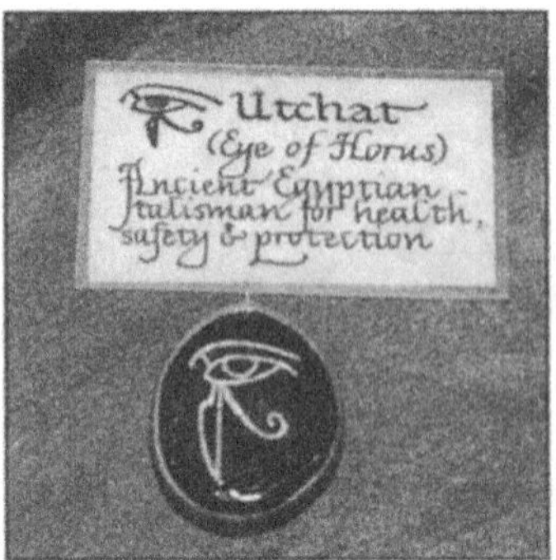

Figure 21. The Ujat, or Eye of Horus amulet; used as a protective charm in ancient Egypt.

he felt he needed to overcome his opponents. He attached it to his lapel with a carnelian lapel pin, carnelian being a stone associated with Mars, the Roman god of victory in battle. The pin appeared attractive and innocuous to his opponents, but it concealed the talisman, which reminded him of his goals and, he believes, helped him to achieve them.

As scholars of folk costume have noted, body adornment can also communicate hierarchy and rank. Gardnerian high priestesses traditionally wear necklaces made of large amber and jet beads, and this custom has spread to other traditions as well. These necklaces have a number of symbolic associations. Amber and jet were once living substances. Because amber consists of fossilized resin, some Pagans consider that all four cardinal elements are involved in its production, lending it special magical and healing properties (Aquino 1998:5). Its golden color is often associated with the sun. Pagans believe jet, which is fossilized lignite, embodies earth energies (Aquino 1998:8). The combination of these gemstones suggests the joining of feminine, earthly, goddess qualities with the masculine, solar attributes of the god in a visual metaphor of the Gardnerian Great Rite, the ritualized union of god and goddess and the central trope for all creativity. The claspless necklaces in alternating colors suggest the never-ending, uninterrupted cycles of life and death. Because necklaces with this combination are difficult to find, many priestesses string their own, using antique or contemporary beads. In a simple necklace strung by Los Angeles artist Raven and her daughter Michele, the beads are left quite deliberately in their natural state, suggesting an immediate connection with nature (fig. 22). Artist April Nino's more elaborate piece alternates carved jet beads and amber, and features a serpent pendant carved in antler, also a symbol of cyclicity and renewal (fig. 23).

Some Wiccan covens have crowns for the high priestess and high priest to wear when they embody the goddess and god during certain rituals. The high priestess's crown usually consists of a circlet with a crescent moon in front, a reference to the goddess Diana, while the high priest's crown has short antlers or horns, symbols of the horned god (fig. 24). Crowns serve a dual function: they indicate to those present that the priestess and priest are embodying the deities, and they can act as important cues that help the wearer slip into the state of divine possession at the appropriate time. The Goddess crown is decorated with symbols of the moon in her three phases (new, full, and waning), which correspond to the three faces of the goddess as maiden, mother, and crone. The god crown has stylized antlers and a crescent moon.

A central icon in jewelry, as in all the movement's ma-

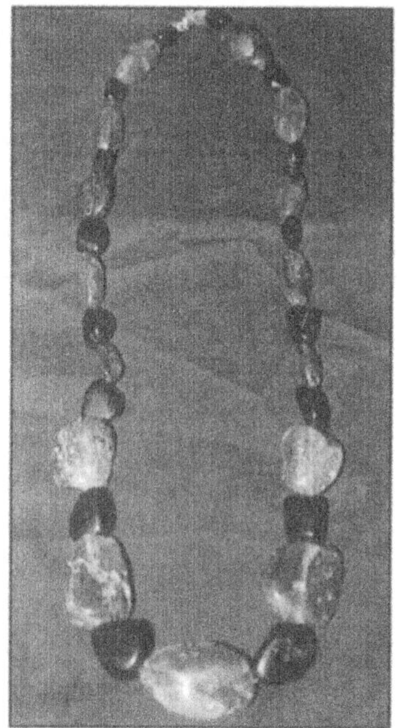

Figure 22. Simple amber and jet necklace, by Raven and Michele of Raven's Flight in North Hollywood, California.

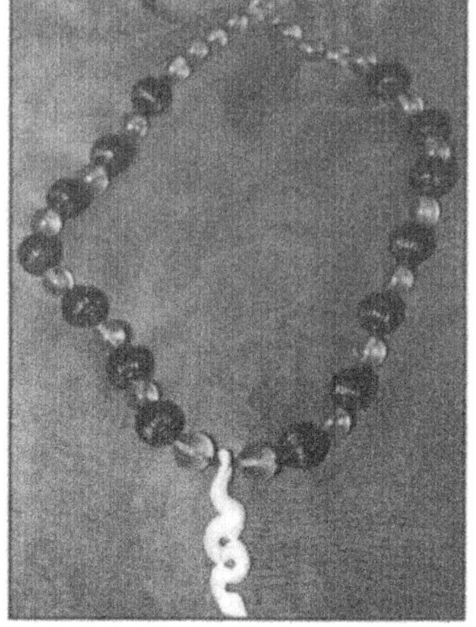

Figure 23. Carved jet and amber necklace with antler serpent, by April Nino. From the collection of Rhiannon.

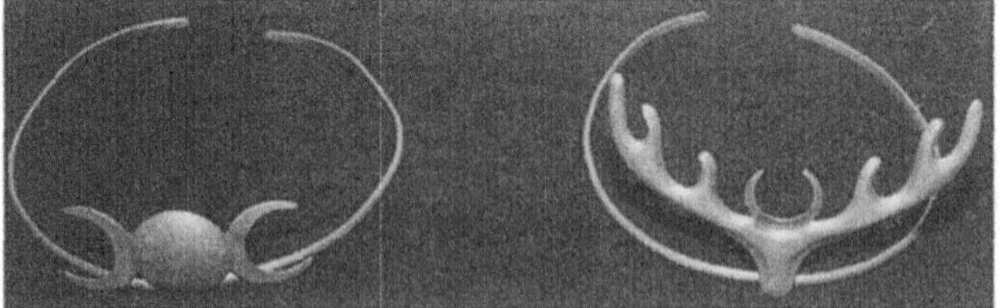

Figure 24. Goddess and god crowns, bronze. From the collection of Arios and Jana of coven Ul.

terial culture, is the female figure. These may take the form of specific goddesses from ancient cultures, but, more commonly, they appear as rounded nudes similar to the Venus of Willendorf and other prehistoric female figurines that Pagans believe represented ancient goddesses.[14] The work of artist Reva Myers is among the most noteworthy in this area. Reva carves her figurines in white-tailed deer antler,[15] fossil tooth,[16] and amber, or casts them in silver, copper, or bronze using the lost wax method. They are typically quite small—two to three inches in length—so that they can either be worn as pendants or mounted as altar pieces. While she has made a variety of pieces representing a range of natural objects and symbols, her most remarkable work is with female and animal figures. She makes a range of female figurines, from rounded nudes reminiscent of prehistoric sculptures, which she calls "Earth Mothers" (plate 13), to the more ethereal, slender "Maiden Goddesses" or "Pretty Ladies," whose outstretched arms seem to be reaching for the sky (plate 14). The figures reveal Reva's extraordinary artistic feeling for the female body in all its diverse forms. "I'm really influenced by the women in my life," she explained. "My sister, . . . she's very inspirational to me, because she's a babe. . . . A babe is the essence of being a powerful woman." Reva studied fine art and art education at the University of Cincinnati before moving west to Arizona and taking up carving. She considers her work to have been profoundly influenced by her Pagan spirituality, both in subject matter and in style: "Almost all the work I do now comes from my spiritual path. . . . I believe that the spark of life is a sacred thing, and everything that's got it, which is everything, . . . we're all tied together, . . . we're not separate. I don't recognize anyone else's power to stand between me and what's sacred; so therefore, what's sacred to me is how I interpret it. . . . When I do ritual I recognize the powers of the various elements in myself and . . . my ties with the rest of the universe. I pray before I sit down to carve or paint every time. I usually call the elements to help me and be present before I work, and I burn sage, and I ground and center. . . . Usually if I sit down to carve something, you know, a raven, say, or a bear, . . . I'll do my ritual, I'll cast my circle and pray to the spirit of that thing. I'll say, 'Spirit of Raven, . . . take form through my hands.'"

Reva often feels that she is simply a channel for a creative power working through her—a force she needs to make room for by disconnecting her intellect and intention from the work. She burns sage or incense before beginning to carve, creating sacred space where she can enter into a prayerful state from which her figures emerge: "When I'm carving, a lot of times I just zone out. I listen to music, and I just try to turn off my brain and let my hands work, and then I'll come back and there'll be a cool carving."

Like Irish, Reva prefers to let the form of her carvings emerge naturally from the material: "I'll sit down and I'll just pick up something and I'll see what I see in there." First, a sander is used to remove the chalky outer coating from fossil teeth, amber, and antlers. Reva then uses a band saw to cut the materials into smaller pieces. She does the bulk of the carving with a Foredom, a jeweler's tool that resembles a dentist's drill, with burrs and bits in different sizes. Each piece is then hand-finished with sandpaper and steel wool, and buffed on a buffing wheel (figs. 25, 26).

Animals, the natural world, and mythology provide the inspiration for many of Reva's pieces. Before carving a set of cat figurines, for example, she looked at pictures of the cat goddess Bast from a book about Egyptian mythology. Yet Reva's cats are not merely replicas of their Egyptian counterparts; they are more animated, with slightly cocked heads, curious expres-

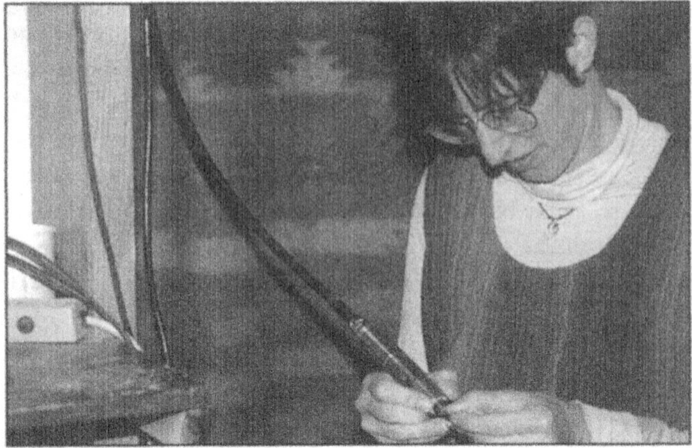

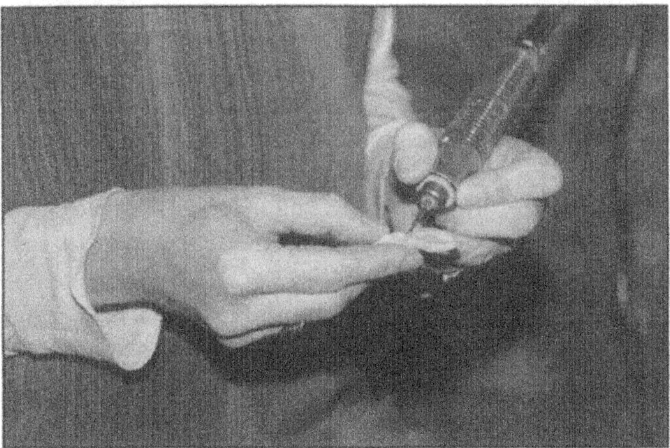

Figures 25 and 26. Reva Myers in her Bisbee, Arizona, workshop. Here she uses a sander to finish a piece carved in antler.

sions, and delicately carved paws and toes underneath (plate 15). Each has its own personality, just as Reva feels each of her own cats has a distinct and individual character. "Dragon Pup" (plate 16), carved from a piece of solid amber, is one of her more spectacular pieces. Larger than usual for her work—about the size of a fist—the curled-up pup has sinuous curves that are intricately carved with tiny, realistic scales. A blue moonstone is set in the center of its forehead like a third eye, indicating its mythological and magical qualities. Yet the pup is as realistic as possible for a mythological animal, its still-unformed face soft in rest like one of the many puppies and kittens lounging around Reva's snug Arizona bungalow. "Dragon Pup" reflects the Pagan belief that magic is a real force in the world; in this religion, the imaginary is not separate from the ordinary, not less real. Even the mythological acquires a reality and integrity that require it to conform to "natural" laws.

Reva's Pagan conception of the interconnected universe is also apparent in her carvings of animal-women (plate 17), which reflect the idea that all life is intertwined, flowing, and essentially composed of the same elements. She has carved wolf-women, lion-women, heron- and raven-women, centaur-women, bat-women (both with folded wings and with out-stretched wings), and women with bird wings, as well as a Selkie, a seal woman from Scottish folklore. She started experi-menting with these hybrid figures after reading Clarissa Pinkola Estés's popular book, *Women Who Run with the Wolves* (1992). Estés explains how, despite her attempts to be a good girl as she was growing up, her (metaphorical) wolf tail kept hanging be-low her dress, giving away her unruly, wild nature (1992:6). This inspired Reva to carve a series of figurines representing a woman's transformation, beginning with a woman howling and ending with a wolf. Reva's wolf-girl (plate 18, right) has the torso of a woman and the legs and tail of a wolf. She crouches, her metamorphosis still in process: one leg is furry, while the other is still womanly, and little ears are beginning to sprout on her head. About the animal-woman figures, Reva says, "They're powerful, and they're comfortable with their wildness. Which is where I think our power comes from: being in touch with that wild part of ourselves."

A great deal of Reva's art is inspired by her personal relation-ships. When I first interviewed her in 1995, she was married and living with her husband and two sons in southern Arizona. She showed me a number of intertwined figures involving a male and female, or two males and a female. In "Karma Divers" (plate 19, top right), two interconnected figures, a male and a female, flow into one another, their interdependence reflecting Reva's view of the powerful emotional entanglements of relationships and the interconnectedness of all life-forms. When I visited her again in the winter of 1998, she was recently divorced and undergoing a period of personal and artistic exploration. She showed me one of her newest pieces, an amber figure of a woman attempting to divine the future by gazing into a bowl (fig. 27). "She's just becoming aware of how her future will go; she hasn't yet decided what to do about it," Reva said of this figure. I could not

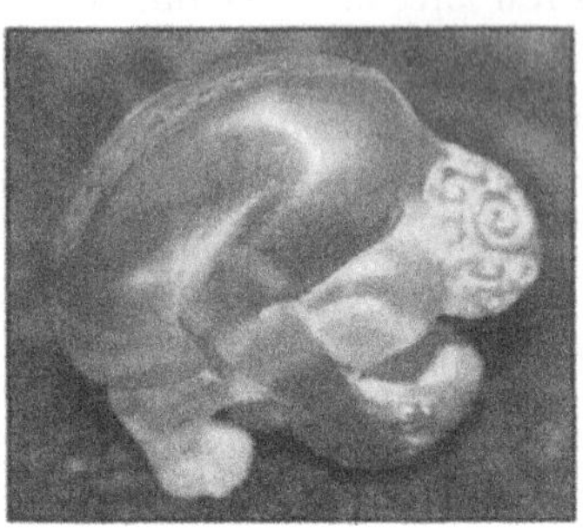

Figure 27. "Scrying woman," amber, by Reva Myers.

help thinking that this woman, with her hair shorn like Reva's own, and who was seeking to forecast her future, represented Reva during this transitional period in her life. She said of her carvings: "[T]hey very often reflect my inner emotional state. When I put these carvings on display, I feel really naked a lot of times."

Reva sells her pieces at Pagan festivals and Renaissance fairs around the West and Southwest. Because her carvings are fairly expensive, she also works in silver, copper, and bronze, using the lost wax method, which is how her bronze altar set (see fig. 10) was made. Many who own her pieces combine them with beads and other charms to create highly personal compositions, often with symbolic meaning and magical intent. Reva considers this the highest compliment: "Truly, that people can touch their own creativity through looking [at] or enjoying or wearing a piece of my work, [that] is what I strive for."

Body Modification

Within the last fifteen years, tattoos and body painting have become increasingly popular in the Pagan community, in part because they have been embraced by youth culture and other communities as symbols of oppositional identity (Hewitt 1997; Wojcik 1995). Designs are often similar to those seen in jewelry: geometric motifs such as spirals, pentagrams, and Celtic knotwork; animals, both real and mythological; and motifs drawn from nature, such as suns, moons, stars, and trees (Pike 1996b:132). Like jewelry, these adornments articulate specific religious identities and express the individual aesthetics of the wearer. One of Sarah Pike's consultants explained the importance of body marking by emphasizing that, in the Pagan community, the unmarked body is the socially undifferentiated body—uncommunicative and apart from the social experience (1996b:132). For some Pagans, the processes of body modification themselves, such as tattooing and piercing, are a source of religious ecstasy and a form of connection to the divine. One northern California festival featured the Ball Dance, a ritual in which participants were pierced with weighted balls that hung through the piercings. They danced ecstatically until the balls ripped out of their flesh. For the participants, the overcoming of pain was a gateway to religious ecstasy, an altered state of consciousness in which they felt joined with the sacred. Because body modifications are permanent, they are chosen to be highly significant, and the process of acquiring them is often ritualized.

Less permanent forms of body modification, such as body painting and henna tattooing, have gained increasing popularity, especially at festivals. Participants can mark their bodies for the duration of the festival, but the tattoos wash off within a week or two, allowing the wearer to return to a "mundane" role without raising eyebrows. Henna is a powdered plant substance that must be mixed with water and is then spread on the skin and left for several hours to dry. After it is removed, it leaves a stain lasting from one to three weeks. Henna tattooing is widespread in India and the Middle East, where it also serves to mark the body for ritual occasions: it is commonly used to decorate a bride's hands before the wedding. Traditional henna tattooing, or *mehndi*, was brought to the United States by south

Asian immigrants. Its adoption by contemporary youth culture and then by the Neo-Pagan movement represents another instance of cultural borrowing in the service of aesthetics.

Henna artist Katya Madrid was born in Leningrad (now St. Petersburg) and came to the United States with her family when she was nine years old. She studied filmmaking and English at Boston University's School of Fine Arts. After moving to Berkeley and working as a camera assistant in the film industry, she decided she needed a change and took up henna art. "It was wonderfully sensual and tactile," she explains. "It was a way to make money, but it was also a way to develop myself artistically." Eventually she founded Hennaglyph, her own henna body art business. Katya buys and mixes the henna herself according to a special recipe she developed, which yields a rich, chocolate color that lasts a long time (two to three weeks) on the skin. The henna is put into plastic bags, which are folded to resemble pastry tubes. The tiny opening in the end of the tube allows her to squeeze out a fine line of henna, which is applied to the skin. The skin is first swabbed with alcohol to remove surface oils which interfere with the dyeing process. The henna goes on as a greenish paste (fig. 28). After being fixed with lemon juice and a sugar-water solution, the paste is left on for up to six hours. It is then washed off, and a dark brown stain remains on the skin. Katya works using a large book of designs, both geometric and representational, drawn from a variety of cultures, but her principal inspiration comes from her "canvas," the individual she is decorating. Like other Pagan artists, she describes her work as being the process of teasing the art form out of the raw materials: "I clear my mind and take a moment or two to meditate. First I size up [my client] in a general way: who are they, what are they wearing now, how are they talking to me, etcetera. Then I look into their eyes: What are they not telling me? Then—and this is critical—I spend some time looking at the part of the body that I plan to draw on. By this point I have a pretty good idea of the size, style, and possibly the theme of the design. . . . Recently I did a piece on a friend's shoulder that wrapped around to the front and reached down

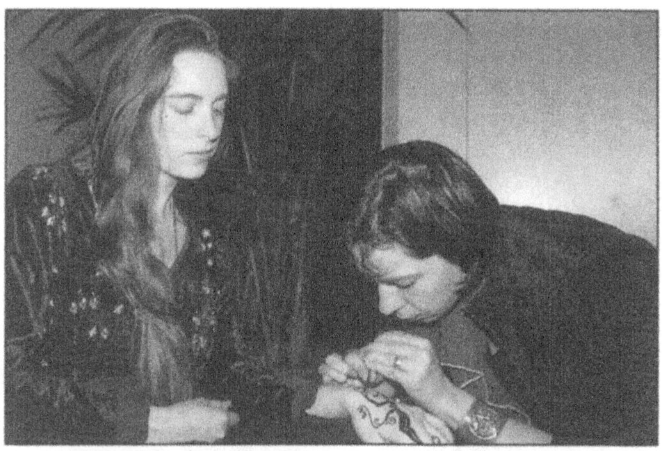

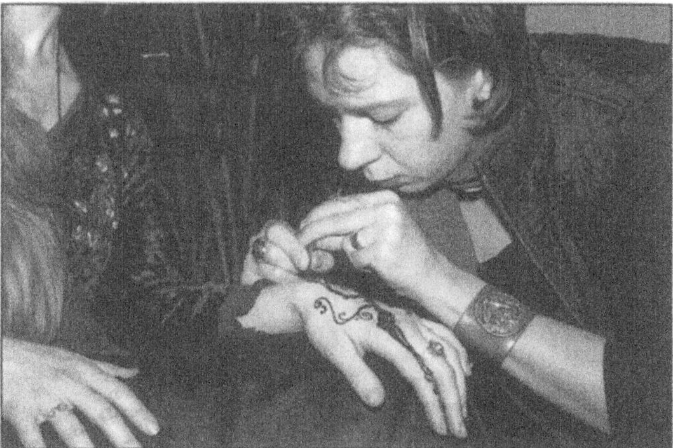

Figures 28 and 29. Katya Madrid applying a henna design to Kore's hand, Pantheacon, San Francisco, February 1999.

to the base of her shoulder blade. . . . Because I know her, I knew what qualities in her personally appealed to me. She is a dancer, so I wanted the piece to be especially graceful. I wanted it to be sexy, but in an elegant way. . . . I wanted a female figure laid out in a slightly angular pose."

Katya turned to art nouveau books and Japanese fabric prints for inspiration, finally settling on Gustav Klimt's painting *Water Serpents* (1904–1907). "What I ended up drawing

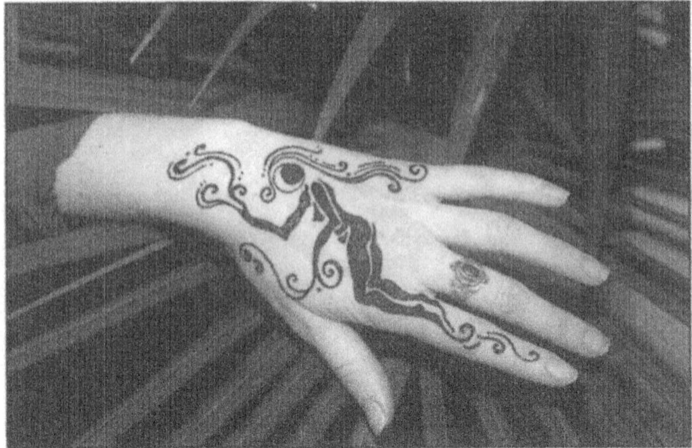

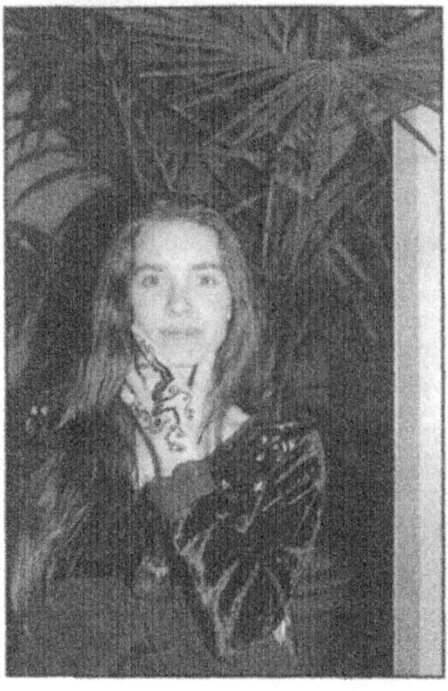

Figures 30 and 31. The completed design shows a moon-headed goddess figure whose hair and limbs form living spirals. Katya described the spirals as "vines, energy—the stuff of life." Spirals are a symbol of the cycle of life, death, and rebirth in Neo-Paganism.

looked nothing like the painting, but I think it inspired a similar emotional response," she explains.

Katya is often asked to decorate someone who is about to undergo an initiation or celebrate a special event, such as a wedding or birthday, or who is expecting a child. "These celebratory reasons mirror the occasions on which henna was and still is done in a traditional context on the Indian subcontinent, in the Middle East, and in Africa, where henna is thought to bring good luck, to be a type of blessing on the skin," she explains. Initiates often choose designs that have a special significance to them, embodying qualities they hope to develop. "[T]here is a magical quality to henna that I believe was understood for hundreds of years which . . . inspired association with good fortune," said Katya. Henna body art can be combined with ritual or magic, incorporating spells, charms, and talismans in both the material and the design. For example, a spell to bring prosperity can be designed to involve decorating the body with symbols of plenty: the symbol for Jupiter (traditionally associated with good luck and prosperity), dollar signs, a cornucopia, and other symbols that suggest abundance. For even greater potency, the henna used in the spell can be mixed with ground herbs associated with Jupiter according to the system of magical correspondences.

Figures 28 and 29 show Katya painting a freehand henna design on the hand of Kore, a Pantheacon participant. "There is an intimacy, both physically and energetically, to painting on the body of another person that [gets] left out of the discussion in the public forum," she explains. "It is more evident if the person that I am working with is spiritual in nature and wants the experience to be special, but it is always present. I look to that person (the subject) for inspiration, and the subject looks at me for an opportunity to express him- or herself through my creativity. A type of symbiotic relationship exists. . . . Two strangers are feeding on, growing from what they create together" (figs. 30, 31).

Ritual Dress and Undress

In his studies of folk costuming in religious communities, Don Yoder observed: "If worship is the 'celebration of life,'[17] in the sense that man dramatizes the wholeness of his life in his festival moods, then festival dress . . . symbolizes this celebration" (1972:305). For Neo-Pagans, ritual dress (and undress) mark the shift from everyday reality to ritual reality. Yoder observed that in traditional religious communities, folk costuming expresses the individual's conforming participation in the community, rather than his/her individuality (1972:308). At first glance, this seems quite uncharacteristic of the Neo-Pagan community, where individuality is highly valued. Yet despite the initial appearance of unbridled creativity and complete freedom, there are rules and guidelines governing Pagan dress. The appearance of rule-breaking in costume is not the same as an absence of rules, as I learned when I first began to attend Neo-Pagan events. In the beginning, I wore my regular street clothes: at festivals, which are usually outdoor camp-outs, I had on shorts and T-shirts; at conferences, I wore what I thought of as a dressed-down version of academic conference garb—twill pants, a blouse, and a tweed jacket. Yet some Pagan acquaintances made fun of my overly academic appearance, and urged me to change into more appropriate attire. I finally bought a long, flowing black silk dress, plain enough not to draw attention but less conspicuously out of place than tweeds. Pagan ritual costuming stands as a critique of the dominant culture, whether it consists of elaborate medieval-looking robes or complete nudity (Pike 1996b:132). Tweeds and "preppy" clothes, as emblems of the elite academic establishment, are inappropriate at a Neo-Pagan event because they represent the very structures the movement tries to oppose. Now, after several years of fieldwork in the Pagan community, I feel strange and out of place wearing street clothes to a festive event, just as I would feel uncomfortable in "witchy" clothes in front of a classroom.

What does Neo-Pagan folk costume look like? There is no single item or combination of items characterizing it; like other aspects of the subculture, it draws from a variety of sources. Medieval and pre-Raphaelite looks predominate, with a dose of Viking and Hollywood Egyptian elements. In some parts of the country, younger Pagans may overlap with "Goths," youth who adopt a theatrical look featuring Romantic clothing and heavy, dark eye makeup against very white skin. Long hair is common for both men and women, and many Pagan men favor beards; everyone wears lots of black, a color traditionally associated with witches in European folklore. Both women and men wear necklaces and pendants in multiples; body paint and tattoos are not uncommon. The overall general effect is one of loose, gentle roguishness.

Like Dick Hebdige's urban youth, Neo-Pagans appropriate elements of costume from many different cultures and symbol systems and manipulate them in ways that oppose the dominant culture's ideas of appropriateness (1987:92). As in the bricolage of symbols which characterizes altars, the signs do not lose their previous associations, but gain new ones in juxtaposition to others. The juxtapositions themselves often are used to highlight social conflicts and contradictions Pagans wish to emphasize. For example, at Pagan festivals, some men wear skirts or sarongs as symbols of protest against traditional male and female gender roles. The wearing of clay or wooden "horns" strapped to the head violates the boundaries between human and animal, and suggests sexuality, devilment, and mischief.

For some followers of Wiccan traditions, nudity itself becomes a form of costuming. Gerald Gardner's Witches practiced their rituals "skyclad" (naked), believing that clothing inhibited the raising of energy from their bodies which was at the core of ritual magic. Gardnerians and certain other British traditionalists continue this practice, though nudity is found only at private coven meetings and closed festivals. For practitioners, it is a powerful expression of the body and its essential sacredness, in direct opposition to Western culture, in which nudity (frequently equated with sexuality) and sacredness are thought of as being at opposite poles. For Gardnerian Witches, nakedness is a symbol of openness and vulnerability before the deities and each other; the naked body is sexual, but not *only* sexual, and sexuality is an expression of the sacred polarity that underlies all life in the universe. Nakedness also removes class differences among participants, itself a form of social critique, and creates a strong sense of intimacy. Coveners who worship naked see each other at their most vulnerable, yet no one leers, stares, or comments; participants are in safe, sacred space. This contributes to the sense of "perfect love and perfect trust" which Wiccans say ideally should prevail in a coven.

Nonetheless, the majority of those worshipping in Neo-Pagan groups wear some sort of clothing. Sometimes this is for practical reasons: at Circle Sanctuary in Wisconsin, where ritu-

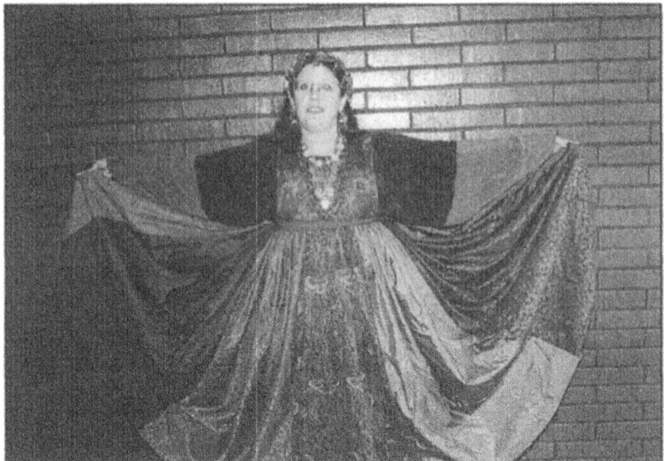

Figure 32. Ellen Perlman wearing her handmade costume embodying the qualities of Melektaus, the blue, or peacock, god of Victor Anderson's Feri Tradition.

als are held outdoors all year long, three-foot-deep snow and temperatures below the freezing mark necessitate parkas, boots, gloves, and warm clothing for much of the year, rather than nudity or elaborate costumes. The development of special ritual clothing parallels the expansion of Paganism beyond Gardnerian Craft and the growth of a public festival culture where aspects of Pagan identity and affiliation can be performed. Like jewelry, costumes communicate important messages about the wearer's tradition, rank, and individual proclivities.

While some Pagans and Witches buy ritual wear or assemble costumes from thrift store finds, many prefer to make their own costumes, thereby controlling the process, achieving exactly the result they want, and imbuing the costume itself with magical energy. Ellen Perlman used the "Folkways" pattern for an Afghani dress to create a costume embodying the qualities of Melektaus, the Blue God (or Peacock God) of Victor Anderson's Feri tradition (fig. 32). According to the teachings of Anderson, a Pagan author, the Blue God is the all-encompassing Star Goddess's first emanation, and her hermaphroditic consort. His qualities include youthfulness and sensuality, and he is sometimes identified with the "god self" or sacred spirit which Anderson and his followers teach is a part of every human being.[18] Ellen chose fabrics in blues, teals, and purples to help her connect with that part of herself when she wears the dress in ritual. The patterns on the fabrics have peacock feathers, butterflies, and orchids printed on them, all symbols connected with the Blue God. Each panel is made of a different fabric that works well with the others. Ellen artfully arranged them so the colors would be gradated, adding to the harmonious quality of the dress.

Ritual garb not only facilitates the expression of individual identity and social critique but can also be used as part of the theatrics of staging a ritual. Some of the most fascinating uses of costume in sacred space involve the hobby horse and teaser costumes of the New Reformed Orthodox Order of the Golden Dawn. NROOGD, a group based in the San Francisco area, holds a large public Beltaine (May 1) ritual each year in a Berkeley park. The ritual is modeled after Padstow, Cornwall's May 1 hobby horse ceremony, recorded on film by Alan Lomax, Peter Kennedy, and Jean Ritchie in *'Oss! 'Oss! Wee 'Oss!* (Folklife Productions, 1953). As in a number of European *quêtes*, or guising traditions, the Padstow 'oss dances through the streets on May Day, followed by musicians, drummers, and members of the 'oss team who stop beneath the windows of prominent citizens to ask for donations with a ritual song. Also as in other guising traditions (Abrahams 1972; Bendix 1985; Bauman 1972; Glassie 1975), the 'oss's visit is believed to bring good luck. The Padstow 'oss is associated with fertility: it chases women and attempts to catch them under its skirt. Padstowers believe that women who touch the 'oss will be married within the year.

The NROOGD reenactment of this tradition was the brainchild of priestesses Leigh Ann Hussey and Laurel Olson. Laurel first learned about the Padstow hobby horse and May Day ritual from a Cornish group participating in the Renaissance Faire in southern California. In her own words, "I fell in love with the horse." Horses are a personal totem for Laurel; throughout her life, she has dreamt of a black horse, especially during times of transition. Because Laurel is of Cornish extraction, the horse is also a symbol of her connection to her ancestral past. She became determined to incorporate a reenactment of the Padstow hobby horse custom as part of NROOGD's public May Day celebration.

The NROOGD custom differs considerably from the Padstow original. The 'oss dances as part of a ritual celebrating Beltaine, or May 1, the beginning of the summer season in the Neo-Pagan year cycle. The ritual takes place entirely in a public park; there is no *quête*, or luck-visiting, through the streets of Berkeley. NROOGD's Beltaine incorporates other revivals of European folk customs, such as maypole dancing and a mock battle between the winter queen and her court and the May queen and her court.[19] But the calling of the 'oss into the sacred circle and the dancing of the 'oss to the traditional Padstow songs is the highlight of the ritual for all those present. After the maypole dance, the teaser, who acts as a guide for the 'oss, moves to the center of the circle. "You know what time it is, don't you?" she tells the anticipating crowd. "It's time to call him—the 'oss!" She moves outside the circle and cries out to the 'oss, who has been hiding behind some bushes, "'Oss, 'oss!" "Wee 'oss!" the crowd responds. The cry is repeated three times; then the 'oss begins to approach from the far end of the field, black skirt and mane flapping in the breeze. From far away, the awkward horse appears powerful and otherworldly (plate 20). The 'oss enters the circle and begins to dance, closely mirroring the teaser's body movements. Because the 'oss is not able to see well from beneath his mask, the teaser's role is crucial in guiding him (fig. 33). As in the Padstow original, contact with the 'oss is thought to bring good luck and fertility: one NROOGD member who was diagnosed as infertile by doctors claimed she conceived after passing under the 'oss's skirt. "Fertility" need not be strictly reproductive; some members feel it also enhances creativity and prosperity on a more abstract level.

NROOGD's hobby horse was first built in 1989 by Leigh Ann Hussey, with the help of Laurel Olson and other members, based on archival photographs of the horse and images from the film. The costume consists of a round framework about six feet in di-

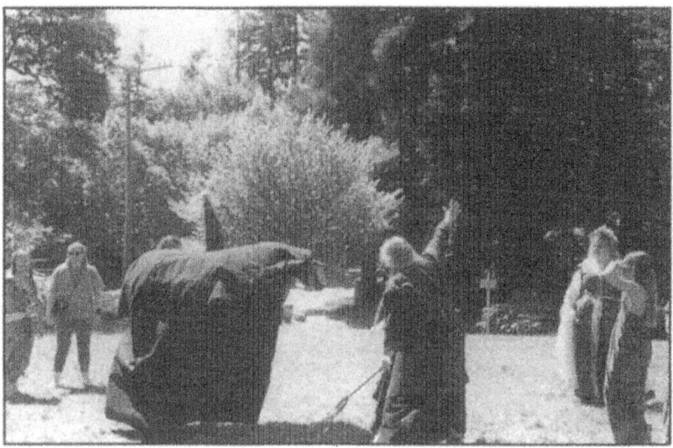

Figure 33. 'Oss and teaser in their mirroring dance, Berkeley, May 1997.

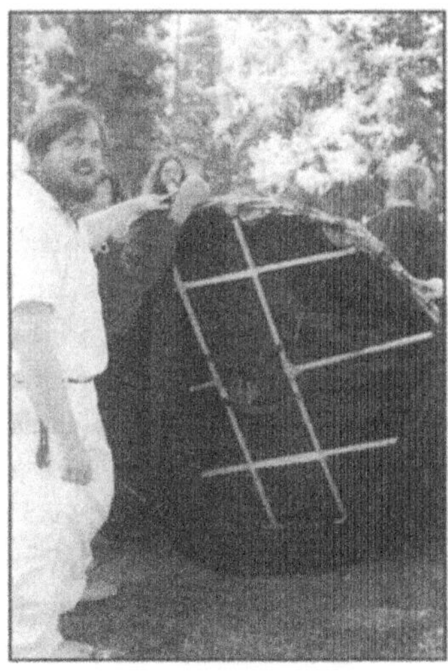

Figure 34. D. H. Frew with framework of the 'oss costume, welded wire and wood covered with cotton, built by Leigh Ann Hussey, Andy Mendez, Laurel Olson, and other NROOGD members.

ameter fitted with leather straps, so it can be worn on the shoulders (fig. 34). The framework is covered with black cotton fabric that hangs down, forming a skirt that covers the horse's legs and falls nearly to the ground. The original framework was made of redwood laths, which had been soaked to render them more flexible, but the laths kept snapping. Gradually, the framework has been replaced with steel conduit woven with steel wire, though the central part of the framework is still made of wooden laths.

Six feet in diameter and weighing over thirty pounds, the costume is extremely heavy and awkward to wear. For this reason, the 'oss has traditionally been played by a man. In figure

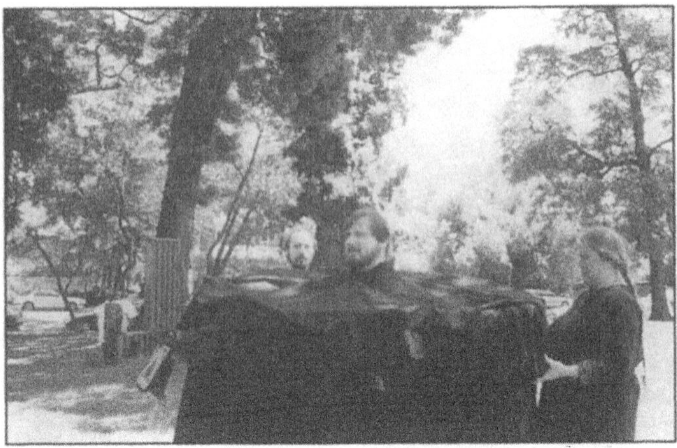

Figure 35. D. H. Frew being helped into 'oss costume by Sam Webster and Laurel Olson, Berkeley, May 1997.

35, Don Frew, the NROOGD elder who played the 'oss from 1989 to 1997, must be helped into his costume by Laurel Olson and Sam Webster. Once in it, his vision and movements are limited.

The most distinctive parts of the costume are the horse's head, mounted on a pole that attaches to the framework, and the conical hat that covers the face of the "rider." The horse's head has "snappers," or hinged jaws that make a snapping sound, as well as a wool "beard," which is designed to catch and fling water during one part of the dance, when the horse is made to "drink" from a bucket (plate 21). The conical cap conceals the identity of the man impersonating the 'oss. Both were painted by Leigh Ann Hussey and are close replicas of the Padstow masks shown in the film.

Laurel Olson has played the teaser to the 'oss since 1990. Her costume, a loose black cotton robe trimmed with red embroidery, and her stick, decorated with red streamers, were designed to complement the red and black of the 'oss costume. Under the 'oss framework, Don is dressed in a white shirt and trousers, with a red neck scarf and cord worn around his waist. He also wears ankle bells, so the 'oss jingles when he walks. Laurel's and Don's costumes were designed to complement each other so the connection between them would still be apparent even when Don was not wearing the 'oss framework. These costumes represent an innovation, for in Padstow the teaser wears street clothes and the man playing the 'oss is not costumed beneath the 'oss framework.

Like other aspects of Neo-Pagan sacred art, the NROOGD 'oss and teaser costumes suggest a connection with a pre-Christian European past preserved in Cornish folk custom. This connection to the past is particularly important in year-cycle rites, as it creates links to historical peoples who celebrated the same customs and emphasizes continuity with them. Yet the NROOGD Beltaine is no mere reenactment; it is a creative adaptation, a new-world bricolage of European folk customs into a new and coherent whole. As Barbara Kirshenblatt-Gimblett observed, traditional folkloric forms have a number of "afterlives" in the late twentieth century (1997). The costumes are crucial both in creating a link with the past and in transporting participants and audience members into the heart of the ritual.

Elemental Masks

Among the more dramatic examples of Neo-Pagan sacred costume art are masks that are used to embody the four sacred elements in the Grand Council meetings of Covenant of the Goddess (COG), a national networking organization of Witches and covens. COG holds its yearly meetings in late August or early September. Member covens send delegates to Grand Council, where the organization's business is conducted by consensus process at lengthy meetings. Since the 1996 meeting, COG has used masks during the meetings. Reclaiming priestess M. Macha NightMare explains the origin and function of this tradition:

In Starhawk's recent novel, *The Fifth Sacred Thing,* masked representatives of the voices of the four elements channeled in trance during council meetings. When I read this idea, I was intrigued by it, so I asked Starhawk if the technique had been tried. She said it hadn't, it was just an idea. . . .

Using mask-wearers to ensure that the proceedings are harmonious with Air, Fire, Water and Earth struck me as a magical undertaking that could enhance our work. Mask-wearers are not direct participants in the meetings. They do not address matters of policy or implementation of projects. They participate in their sacred capacity as voices of Wind, Fire, Water or Earth. Sometimes they may speak or gesture, and sometimes they merely remain alert. When Wind has something to say, the meeting ceases while Wind speaks. Then the meeting resumes, taking into account the spoken words of Wind. (1998:44)

The first masks were made in 1996 by sculptor Eleanor Myers, an artist associated with the Reclaiming tradition in San Francisco. She drew her original inspiration from Zuni *shakalo* masks, but the finished products were quite different, and did not attempt to re-create or reproduce an authentic Zuni design. She crafted them from found materials: recycled cardboard shaped into cylinders, a hubcap, rusted metal parts and wires, branches and moss. The masks were heavy, cylindrical, and brownish, designed to rest on the shoulders of the wearers, with small eye slits; their overall appearance was "chthonic" (NightMare 1998:45). Some wearers observed that the placement of the eye openings created an atmosphere inside the mask that eased the wearer into a trance state (NightMare 1998:48). On several occasions during the 1996 Grand Council, the masked representatives of the Mighty Ones spoke, though at times the exact meaning of their utterances was opaque. NightMare observed that "Christopher, who was an active participant . . . remarked . . . that this was just how the ancient oracles operated. . . . " (1998:47).

This custom was received with so much acclaim by COG members that it was decided to continue the tradition. In 1998, Jana and Arios, Gardnerian practitioners and COG members from San Francisco, created new element masks along with members of their coven. Jana decided to make the masks in the forms of animals: a bird for air/east, a fire-cat for fire/south, a fish for water/west, and a bear for earth/north (plates 22–25).

"My goal," explained Jana, "was to help create a direct experience [for the participant/users] of an elemental force, to encourage an ecstatic state and a sense of communion. I also hoped the wearers could convey this otherworldliness to Grand Council."

Like other Pagan artists, Jana sees the act of creation as sacred. "For me to be able to work artistically, I have to be able to create sacred art," she explained. Regardless of the medium, she said, "It's all sacred to me." (She also belly dances, paints, and designs and makes costumes.) Art is especially important to her as a medium for bringing a sense of sacredness to others. Jana defined the sacred as "a sense of oneness with the universe, a sense of the sacredness of the self, of others, of things of the earth—whether it's a river or a rock or an animal; and of the supernatural: both the powerful elemental forces and the 'little gods' we Witches work with, the anthropomorphized gods."

She chose to make the element masks in the shapes of animals in order to emphasize the connection of the elements with the natural world. In a letter, she wrote, "All four animals are from Europe. I see Witchcraft as European shamanism (among other things), and in order to convey this, I decided to be Euro-centric in . . . choosing which animals to use. I was also trying to stay away from the Biblical four (Lion, Eagle, Bull and Man). Bear, Eagle, Cat and Fish are what came out of this. . . . For all four animals, I tried to convey an 'all-bear,' 'all-bird' (OK, bird of prey), 'all-cat,' 'all-fish' [feeling], so that anyone wearing the mask could find their own special connection to the power that each represents."

In preparation for the mask making, Jana and her coven did research on each animal, looking at photographs and "anthropomorphizing the forms somewhat to make the connection between animal, element, and person." Jana, Arios, and the other members of coven Ul worked cooperatively on the project, so that the masks represent a communal as well as a magical creation. The face plates were made first, from plaster strips molded over plastic or aluminum foil foundations. D rings were attached to the back so the knotted headdress could be added later. Then the face plates were painted, and feathers were applied to the bird mask. Next, Jana hand-dyed the rope she would use to crochet the headdress portion of each mask. She used different sizes and textures of rope for each animal: "[T]he bear is very loose and a very large gauge of rope, [while] the bird, which is tight and dense, is woven in a pattern to convey wings and tail feathers." The knotwork on the fish mask suggests scales and tentacles, emphasizing its nature as a sea creature rather than as one specific type of fish (plate 24).

Jana feels a strong sense of connection with her creations, which she refers to as "my babies," as though they came "through" her apart from her conscious volition. She believes each one has its own personality: "The bird feels very serious and scholarly to me; the cat jumpy, exploratory, and action-oriented; the fish mystical and otherworldly; the bear grounded and humorous." Their characters are connected to the elemental qualities each animal embodies: thought (air), courage (fire), feeling and reflection (water), and practicality (earth).

Jana remarked, "Masks are great for allowing people to become other than themselves. Even shy people, costumed, are able to leave their mundane selves and travel to different places, embody [or] be possessed by other spirits." Like the crowns worn by Gardnerian priestesses and priests while "drawing down" or channeling the deities, the masks act as cues for the wearers to enter an altered state of consciousness. Many who wore the masks during Grand Council reported feelings of being in a light trance, alert yet somehow removed from the proceedings. Wearers also felt connected to the elemental forces and the qualities they embodied; when they were moved to speak, they often did so from the point of view of that particular elemental force. In this way, Wiccans in COG quite literally bring the sacred into the mundane space of their yearly business meetings, sacralizing a potentially boring and tedious event by connecting it to the natural and divine forces around them.

CONCLUSION

All religion has traditionally included visual experiences as well as purely spiritual ones, and all religions make use of symbols to illustrate fundamental spiritual values and principles. Is it possible, from this brief overview of Neo-Pagan art, to arrive at an articulation of the movement's aesthetics, or at conclusions about its developing iconography? What, if anything, can all these disparate forms be said to have in common? How are Neo-Pagan and Wiccan visual representations different from those of the dominant religions in the United States?

As Michael Owen Jones wrote in his seminal essay on folk aesthetics, "[I]n regard to any group's art forms there is probably no extensive system of verbalized aesthetic principles codified into a canon transmitted and guarded by a group of critics" (1971:104). This is especially true of a decentered and individualistic movement like contemporary Paganism and revival Witchcraft, where the very notion of a central authority determining the aesthetic standard of creative works is anathema. Yet as Jones suggests, aesthetic principles are often "embedded in traditional and conventionalized forms of expression" (1971:104). While each artist or small group of artists I have examined works individually, their vision, iconography, and aesthetics are not private or individual, but communal and shared. Their works reflect a shared worldview that is intimately related to the politics of the movement as a whole.

Central to Neo-Pagan aesthetics is attention to subject matter and form. The movement is creating its own iconography intentionally oppositional to that of the dominant Christianity of North America. The overarching theme of much Neo-Pagan sacred art focuses on the reconnection of humans with the sacred, which is seen as immanent in nature and elemental forces. Neo-Pagan sacred art rejects the Augustinian notion of nature and the human body as temporal, flawed, and corrupt. Instead, nature is idealized, humans are portrayed as inseparable from nature, and the entire universe is imagined as interconnected through a system of symbolic correspondences. Metonymy, in which a part associated with an element suggests the whole, with all of its associated correspondences, is a common trope in Neo-Pagan sacred art.

The subject matter of a great deal of Neo-Pagan art is the natural world in its many forms: plant, animal, and celestial motifs and symbols as well as the human, especially the feminine, figure. The idea of the feminine divine is primary in the movement; not only are women viewed as the embodiment of the goddess, but reproduction is seen as the central metaphor for all creativity. It is not surprising that the movement has so many good women artists. The feminine divine is represented in a wide diversity of forms, reflecting a broad range of qualities and attributes, from fierce armed goddesses like Brigid, of holy well and smithy, to pregnant earth mothers to maidens reaching for the heavens to animal-women—icons in which women can see their own individual qualities reflected. These forms have a Carnivalesque quality to them, in that they transgress Classical notions of the composed, harmonious body which predominate in both Christian and capitalist representations of women. Unlike the waif-thin images in fashion magazines, Pagan representations of the feminine are fleshy, abundant, exuberant, pregnant, morphing into plants and animals; they violate neat and ordered categories of human and animal, cultural and natural. While these images reproduce the paradigm of woman as close to nature, wild, and uncontrollable, which is fundamental to Western culture (Tiffany and Adams 1985), they flip the valence, so that nature (and by association the feminine) becomes positive, sacred, and exalted instead of debased, corrupt, corporeal, and dangerous.

The male deity is not portrayed as often, and god forms are less varied and complex than goddess forms, often being limited to depictions of the horned god in his various guises (Cernunnos, Pan) and the Green Man vegetation deity.[20] Perhaps this situation reflects the difficulties within the movement in thinking about (lowercase) god without relying on images from Christianity—bearded fathers with a whip in one hand and a lollipop in the other, suffering sons, innocent babes in a manger—or on those of excessively martial pagan gods. Coming up with satisfying god images is especially tricky given the questions in the movement about appropriate masculine roles and behaviors: there is a rejection of hypermasculinity and the "tough guy" image, but no clear new models of what it means to be a man. Still, like their feminine counterparts, images of male divinity merge the human and the natural worlds. These horned or leafy figures are intended to act as bridges between humans and nature, emphasizing the presence of the sacred in the natural, the corporeal, and the interconnectedness of the universe.

Since divinity is immanent in all natural forms, the natural form contains perfection. The natural, unaltered form of raw material is thought to have aesthetic and sacred value even without human manipulation and intervention. The role of the artist is to bring forth the sacredness of the material, to reveal its spirit, rather than to alter its basic qualities in some way. At the same time, the creative act is highly valued in this culture. The process of creating art, of transformation, is seen as one kind of magic; therefore, all artistic acts intrinsically have merit, and all artists are essentially magicians or shamans who mediate between the everyday world and the world of the unconscious.

Irish Clark-Savage, Oberon Zell, Reva Myers, Katya Madrid, and Jana all described feeling that their artwork came "through" them from some sacred place outside their conscious minds, apart from their own volition or control. To create art is to do magic, to be actively engaged with the sacred. Because of the sacredness of the creative process and the belief that all individuals have access to it, Neo-Pagan aesthetics are also profoundly egalitarian; the art of a trained professional is not seen as intrinsically more valuable than that of an amateur. In many cases, communal creation is the preferred mode of operation, as when a coven cooperates in the sacred act of making an altar or a set of masks.

Another common theme is the incorporation of motifs, images, and techniques borrowed from the historical past or from the art of non-Western peoples. As Janis Edwards suggests in reference to contemporary feminist art, these tropes "evoke the mysticism of unfamiliar rituals and a visceral sense that so-called 'primitive' cultures are more bound to their religious and spiritual essences than are First World industrial cultures" (1994:41). The incorporation of these images and techniques is part of a yearning for a more authentic sense of connection to deity, environment, and community. Pagans have been criticized for appropriating materials from other cultures without permission, particularly by Native Americans and African Americans, members of cultures that have already suffered exploitation by whites (Eller 1995:77). There is some validity to this critique. The appropriation of motifs from indigenous cultures reduces them to icons of "primitiveness" and their bearers to "noble savages" who embody ancient wisdom and live close to the earth. This representation flattens real cultural difference, both between Euro-Americans and the Other, and among the many different Native American and African ethnic groups, by reducing human beings to symbols. Another common criticism centers around whites' attempts to capitalize on imitations of indigenous artwork at the expense of native peoples themselves. As Cynthia Eller illustrates, Pagans have a range of responses to such accusations, from painstaking attempts to remain completely within their own ethnic heritage to what she calls the "grab-bag approach" (1995:75), justified with various rationalizations. But in the case of Neo-Pagan sacred art, the vast majority of borrowings are from ancient cultures, whose denizens are not around to protest the use of motifs from their traditions. Typically, borrowings do not take the form of exact reproduction; the aim is not to imitate or defraud but to combine elements from different sources to create a new, coherent whole. In this respect, Neo-Pagan sacred art is much like Neo-Pagan ritual (Magliocco 1996); the themes of recombination and reinterpretation are common to all forms of sacred art in the movement. As in ritual, the aim is to heal in the literal sense of "making whole"—creating a whole from separate, unconnected parts. This process is at the core of many different kinds of artistic activities; as Hebdige explains in his study of emerging punk and other youth cultures during the 1980s, "[B]oth artistic expression and aesthetic pleasure are intimately bound up with the destruction of existing codes and the formulation of new ones" (1987:124).

Perhaps a more fruitful way of understanding this impulse is suggested by George Lipsitz's work on popular music, another artistic genre that easily crosses cultural boundaries. He argues that transnationalism and globalization have brought Americans an awareness of the multiplicity of viewpoints—cultural, linguistic, sexual, religious—in the world and a realization of the limits of monolithic institutions such as church and state (1994:10–11). The rebirth of polytheism reflects this refraction of perspective. Borrowing from other cultures may be one way of trying to incorporate, rather than rejecting, this growing diversity. Other spiritual and artistic traditions are seen as having greater potential for multiple viewpoints than those of mainstream Christian traditions, and this is part of their appeal to Neo-Pagans. In her discussion of hybridization, Deborah Kapchan invites us to consider aesthetic hybridizations, such as Pagan icons that combine influences from several different sources, and their relationship to hybridization at larger social, economic, and historical levels (1993:306). Borrowings and appropriations in Pagan art can be seen as reflecting the larger forces of globalization and transnationalism that make available to middle-class Americans a vast range of images from a variety of cultures and historical periods.

As de Certeau suggests, this type of meaning-making activity is particularly characteristic of postmodernity, with its multiplicity of disconnected images and forms (1984). In their sacred art, Neo-Pagans draw from this multiplicity of sources to create new symbolic meanings that explain the social world and imagine a better one, literally and figuratively making things whole. Neo-Pagans are engaged in creating a new and vibrant folk culture through their sacred art. Their art and altars illustrate folklore's central role in creating both individuality and community, a particularly important factor in cases of emergent cultures in which traditions are being invented and community is still largely imagined. Ultimately, the delight that Neo-Pagans take in all forms of artistic expression and in the artistic process itself can enlighten us about the reasons individuals may be drawn to this oppositional religious movement. Neo-Pagans have re-created, in a postmodern context, the ethos of the traditional preindustrial community in which all members were folk artists of some sort. They value the folkloric process not only because it recalls the ethos of the past or is a vehicle for critiquing the dominant culture, but because the process of creation is pleasurable in and of itself. The artistic process is perceived as a kind of magic, a transformation, a path to union with the sacred. Sacred art is healing in the most basic sense of the word: making things whole.

ΠΟΤΕΣ

1. The term was coined by Tim "Oberon" (previously "Otter") Zell, founder of the Church of All Worlds, but contemporary Pagans often refer to themselves simply as "Pagans," emphasizing their connection to indigenous nature religions and to pre-Christian pagans. I will use the two terms interchangeably in this essay. I capitalize "Witch" and "Witchcraft" when refering to the modern religion, but use the lowercase when employing the terms historically or anthropologically.

2. D. H. Frew (1998) maintains that Kelly's claims against Gardner are specious, and argues persuasively that while no one has ever been able to prove Gardner's claims, there are no significant proofs against them, either.

3. For a provocative exposé of some of the more misogynistic goddess-worshipping traditions, see Jencson (1998).

4. The "Craft Laws," a set of principles in the Gardnerian Book of Shadows (a collection of liturgical materials handed down in strict succession from Gerald B. Gardner's coven in the 1950s to all existing covens that trace their descent from his), prohibit the charging of money for magical instruction but allow the sale of magical tools and objects.

5. Most scholars feel that Gardner and his followers were extremely influential in the standardization and diffusion of twentieth-century revival Witchcraft. Almost all contemporary Witchcraft traditions have been influenced to some extent by Gardner's writings, and many Neo-Pagan traditions have, as well.

6. Pagan and Wiccan traditions differ in the symbolic associations they attribute to various altar tools. Gardnerian, Alexandrian, NROOGD, and Feri traditions, among others, use blades to symbolize fire and wands to symbolize air, while Reclaiming and Church of All Worlds use blades to symbolize air.

7. The inclusion of the four cardinal directions (north, east, south and west) and the elements associated with them comes to Witchcraft from medieval ceremonial magic, in which the directions and the winds corresponding to them were invoked as protective forces to enclose the entities the magicians were summoning. The forms have survived, but the contemporary interpretation is different from the medieval one. Many Witches see the four elements as symbolic of the basic components of nature. Their function is no longer to protect against potentially malevolent entities, but to recognize and honor the natural world of which we are all a part.

8. See Scalora (1997:63–81) for a thorough discussion of the origins and practice of the Mexican custom.

9. See Lafferty (1998:142–45) for an account of how one Mexican-American woman combined family traditions with new practices in creating ancestor altars for Samhain.

10. Oberon Zell, interview by author, February 13, 1999.

11. Ibid.

12. I am indebted to Bill Kilborn for the information that follows. His essay on the history of the pentagram can be found at <http://www.journey1.org/basic-pentagram.htm>.

13. A popular book among Neo-Pagans is Ted Andrews's *Animal-Speak: The Spiritual and Magical Powers of Creatures Great and Small*, which includes dictionaries of mammal, bird, reptile, and insect totems and their symbolic associations.

14. There has been a great deal of debate among archeologists as to the meaning of these figures. While most believe their meaning and function remain unclear, others, especially the popularizer Marija Gimbutas, have interpreted such figures as evidence of early goddess-worshipping matriarchies, a theory that has been adopted as sacred narrative by many Neo-Pagans. See Gimbutas (1994:24–31), Adler (1994:127–37), Eller (1995), and Nelson (1990).

15. White-tailed deer naturally shed their antlers each year. These materials are collected and sold by dealers.

16. "Fossil teeth" are Alaskan walrus and whale teeth between ten thousand and fifty thousand years old. They are not truly fossilized in the geological sense. Only Eskimo and Inuit can collect these materials, which they sell to gem dealers, who in turn sell them to artists like Reva.

17. Von Ogden Vogt, 1929, *Art and Religion*, quoted in Yoder (1972:305).

18. Anderson's Feri tradition teaches that all humans have three selves: "primal self," a younger, nonverbal, nonrational self; "talking self," the rational, logical, conscious ego; and "god self," a higher, spiritual form of the self, often identified with the Blue God.

19. The contemporary NROOGD Beltaine is actually a fusion of two NROOGD covens' previous May Day traditions, one incorporating the 'oss, the other focusing on maypole dancing and the May queen. The two rituals were combined to avoid giving one coven's ritual precedence over another's.

20. Very different images of the god do appear in the mysteries of a number of initiatory traditions, e.g., Gardnerian Wicca, but these depictions are secret and are not part of a public tradition of Neo-Pagan art.

REFERENCES

Abrahams, Roger. 1972. "Christmas and Carnival in St. Vincent." *Western Folklore* 31: 275–89.

Adler, Margot. 1986 [1979]. *Drawing Down the Moon.* Boston: Beacon Press.

———. 1994. "Meanings of Matriarchy." In *The Politics of Women's Spirituality,* ed. Charlene Spretnak, 127–37. New York: Anchor Doubleday.

Andrews, Ted. 1993. *Animal-Speak: The Spiritual and Magical Powers of Creatures Great and Small.* St. Paul: Llewellyn Press.

Appadurai, Arjun. 1986. "Introduction: Commodities and the Politics of Value." In *The Social Life of Things: Commodities in Cultural Perspective.* Cambridge: Cambridge University Press.

Aquino, Donna. 1998. "The Halloween Necklace: Reflections on Amber and Jet." *The Hidden Path* 21, no. 3: 5–9.

Baker, James W. 1996. "White Witches: Historic Fact and Romantic Fantasy." In *Magical Religions and Modern Witchcraft,* ed. James R. Lewis, 171–92. Albany: SUNY Press

Bauman, Richard. 1972. "Belsnickling in a Nova Scotia Island Community." *Western Folklore* 31: 229–43.

Beezley, William H. 1997. "Home Altars: Private Reflections of Public Life." In *Home Altars of Mexico,* ed. Dana Salvo, 91–109. Albuquerque: University of New Mexico Press.

Bendix, Regina. 1985. *Progress and Nostalgia: Silvesterklausen in Urnaesch, Switzerland.* Berkeley: University of California Folklore & Mythology Studies, vol. 33.

Bogatyrev, Peter. 1971 [1937]. *The Function of Folk Costume in Moravian Slovakia.* Trans. Richard Crum. The Hague: Mouton.

Bonewitz, Isaac. 1989. *Real Magic.* York Beach, ME: Samuel Weiser Press.

Bowman, Marion. 1996. "Cardiac Celts: Images of Celts in Paganism." In *Paganism Today,* ed. G. Harvey and C. Hardman, 242–51. San Francisco: Harper Collins.

Brown, Karen. 1990. *Mama Lola: A Vodou Priestess in Brooklyn.* Berkeley: University of California Press.

Cantwell, Robert. 1993. *Ethnomimesis: Folklife and the Representation of Culture.* Chapel Hill: University of North Carolina Press.

Carpenter, Dennis D. 1996. "Practitioners of Paganism and Wiccan Spirituality in Contemporary Society: A Review of the Literature." In *Magical Religions and Modern Witchcraft,* ed. James R. Lewis, 373–405. Albany: SUNY Press.

Carson, Anne. 1992. *Goddesses and Wise Women: The Literature of Feminist Spirituality, 1980–1992. An Annotated Bibliography.* Freedom, CA: The Crossing Press.

Certeau, Michel de. 1984. *The Practice of Everyday Life.* Berkeley: University of California Press.

Chapman, Malcolm. 1992. *The Celts: The Construction of a Myth.* Berkeley: University of California Press.

Edwards, Janis L. 1994. "Spiritual Depictions in Art and the Creation of Female Culture." *Women and Language* 16, no. 1: 40–43.

Eller, Cynthia. 1995. *Living in the Lap of the Goddess: The Feminist Spirituality Movement in America.* Boston: Beacon Press.

Estés, Clarissa P. 1992. *Women Who Run with the Wolves: Myths and Stories of the Wild Woman Archetype.* New York: Ballantine Books.

Farrar, Janet, and Stewart Farrar. 1989. *The Witches' God.* Blaine, WA: Phoenix Publishing.

———. 1987. *The Witches' Goddess.* Blaine, WA: Phoenix Publishing.

Fernandez, James W. 1974. "The Mission of Metaphor in Expressive Culture." *Current Anthropology* 15: 119–45.

Frew, Donald H., III. 1998. "Methodological Flaws in Recent Studies of Historical and Modern Witchcraft." *Ethnologies* 20, no. 1: 33–65.

Gardner, Gerald B. 1973 [1954]. *Witchcraft Today.* Seacaucus, NJ: Citadel Press.

———. 1959. *The Meaning of Witchcraft.* London: Aquarium Press.

Geertz, Clifford. 1973. "Religion as a Cultural System." In *The Interpretation of Cultures,* 87–125. New York: Basic Books.

Gimbutas, Marija. 1994. "Women and Culture in Goddess-Oriented Old Europe." In *The Politics of Women's Spirituality,* ed. Charlene Spretnak, 22–31. New York: Anchor Doubleday.

Glassie, Henry. 1975. *All Silver and No Brass.* Bloomington: Indiana University Press.

Grimes, Ronald L. 1990. *Ritual Criticism.* Columbia, SC: University of South Carolina Press.

Hebdige, Dick. 1987. *Subculture: The Meaning of Style.* London: Routledge.

Hewitt, Kim. 1997. *Mutilating the Body: Identity in Blood and Ink.* Bowling Green, OH: Bowling Green State University Press.

Jencson, Linda. 1998. "In Whose Image? Misogynist Trends in the Construction of Goddess and Woman." In *Spellbound: Women and Witchcraft in*

America, ed. Elizabeth Reis, 247–67. Wilmington, DE: Scholarly Resources.

Jones, Leslie. 1994. "The Emergence of the Druid as Celtic Shaman." In *The Marketing of Tradition: Perspectives in Folklore, Tourism and the Heritage Industry*, ed. Teri Brewer, 131–42. Middlesex: Hisarlik Press.

Jones, Michael Owen. 1971. "The Concept of 'Aesthetic' in the Traditional Arts." *Western Folklore* 30, no. 2: 77–104.

Kapchan, Deborah. 1993. "Hybridization and the Marketplace: Emerging Paradigms in Folkloristics." *Western Folklore* 52, no. 2–4: 303–26.

Kelly, Aidan. 1991. *Crafting the Art of Magic, Book I.* St. Paul, MN: Llewellyn Press.

Kirschenblatt-Gimblett, Barbara. 1997. "Afterlives." *Performance Research* 5: 1–9.

Lafferty, Anne. 1998. "How We Braid Our Lives Together with Our Ancestors." *Ethnologies* 20, no. 1: 129–49.

Lipsitz, George. 1994. *Dangerous Crossroads: Popular Music, Postmodernism, and the Politics of Place.* New York: Verso.

Luhrmann, T. M. 1989. *Persuasions of the Witches' Craft.* Cambridge: Harvard University Press.

Magliocco, Sabina. 1996. "Ritual Is My Chosen Art Form: The Creation of Ritual as Folk Art Among Contemporary Pagans." In *Magical Religions and Modern Witchcraft*, ed. James R. Lewis, 93–120. Albany: SUNY Press.

McMann, Jean. 1998. *Altars and Icons: Sacred Spaces in Everyday Life.* San Francisco: Chronicle Books.

Murray, Margaret. 1952 [1931]. *The God of the Witches.* Oxford: Oxford University Press.

Nelson, Sarah M. 1993. "Diversity in Upper Paleolithic 'Venus' Figurines and Archeological Mythology." In *Gender in Cross-Cultural Perspective*, ed. C. Brettell and C. Sargent, 67–74. Upper Saddle River, NJ: Prentice-Hall.

NightMare, M. Macha (Aline O'Brien). 1998. "Masks in Magical Meetings." *The Pomegranate* 4: 44–49.

Orion, Loretta. 1995. *Never Again the Burning Times: Paganism Revived.* Prospect Heights, IL: Waveland Press.

Pike, Sarah. 1996a. "Rationalizing the Margins: A Review of the Legitimation and Ethnographic Practice in Scholarly Research on Neo-Paganism." In *Magical Religions and Modern Witchcraft*, ed. James R. Lewis, 353–74. Albany: SUNY Press.

———. 1996b. "Forging Magical Selves: Gendered Bodies and Ritual Fires at Neo-Pagan Festivals." In *Magical Religions and Modern Witchcraft*, ed. James R. Lewis, 121–40. Albany: SUNY Press.

Rose, Elliott. 1962. *A Razor for a Goat: A Discussion of Certain Problems in the History of Witchcraft and Diabolism.* Toronto: University of Toronto Press.

Russo, Mary. 1986. "Female Grotesques: Carnival and Theory." In *Feminist Studies, Critical Studies*, ed. Teresa de Lauretis, 213–29. Bloomington: Indiana University Press.

Scalora, Salvatore. 1997. "Flowers and Sugar Skulls for the Spirits of the Dead." In *Home Altars of Mexico*, ed. Dana Salvo, 63–81. Albuquerque: University of New Mexico Press.

Spretnak, Charlene, ed. 1994 [1982]. *The Politics of Women's Spirituality.* New York: Anchor Doubleday.

Starhawk (Miriam Simos). 1989 [1979]. *The Spiral Dance.* San Francisco: Harper Collins.

Tiffany, Sharon W., and Kathleen J. Adams. 1985. *The Wild Woman: An Inquiry into the Anthropology of an Idea.* Cambridge, MA: Schenckman Publishing.

Turner, Kay F. 1999. *Beautiful Necessity: The Art and Meaning of Women's Altars.* New York: Thames and Hudson.

———. 1990. "Mexican-American Women's Home Altars: The Art of Relationship." Ph.D. diss., University of Texas, Austin.

Turner, Victor. 1968. *The Ritual Process.* Ithaca: Cornell University Press.

Valiente, Doreen. 1989. *The Rebirth of Witchcraft.* Custer, WA: Phoenix Press.

Wojcik, Daniel. 1995. *Punk and Neo-Tribal Body Art.* Jackson, MS: University Press of Mississippi.

Yoder, Don. 1972. "Folk Costume." In *Folklore and Folklife: An Introduction,* ed. Richard M. Dorson, 295–323. Chicago: University of Chicago Press.

Zell, Oberon (Tim), Morning Glory Zell, and Liza Gabriel. 1998. "The Millenial Gaia." Pamphlet. Pengrove, CA: Theagenesis LLC.

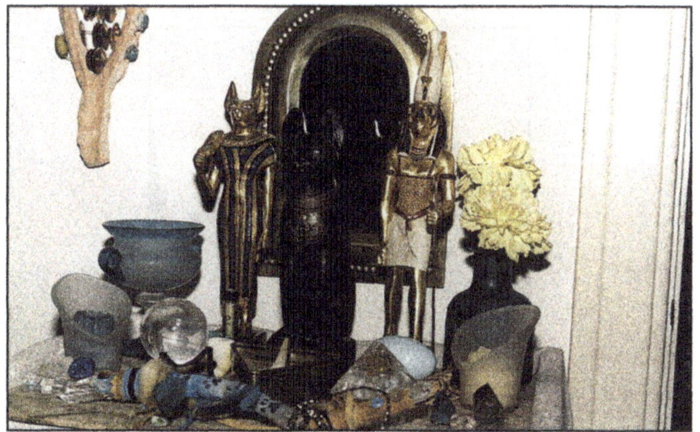

Plate 1. Working altar to Bast and Horus, by Catherine Farah. The altar also holds a crystal-tipped, double-headed wand Catherine made from driftwood; it is decorated with leather, fur bits, feathers, and shiny threads—all materials that appeal to cats—and is painted blue, a color she associates with Bast. Note also the cat pawprints painted on the wand. The object on the wall to the left of the altar is a clay sistrum, a rattle carried by priestesses of Bast and Isis in Egyptian iconography; it was made by Karen Tate.

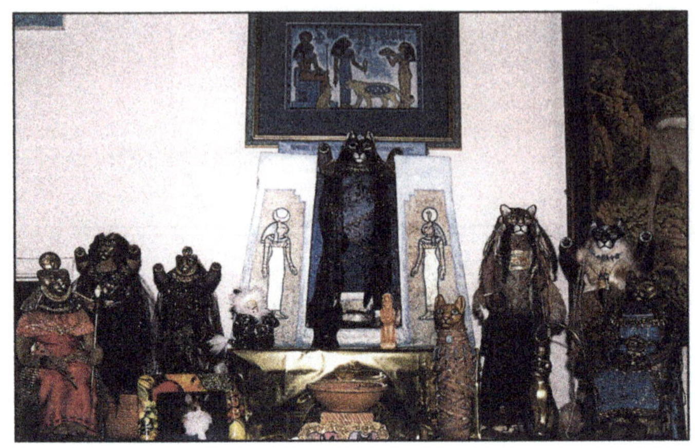

Plate 2. Karen Tate's altar to Bast. The cat figures by Catherine Farah look over photos of Karen's cats.

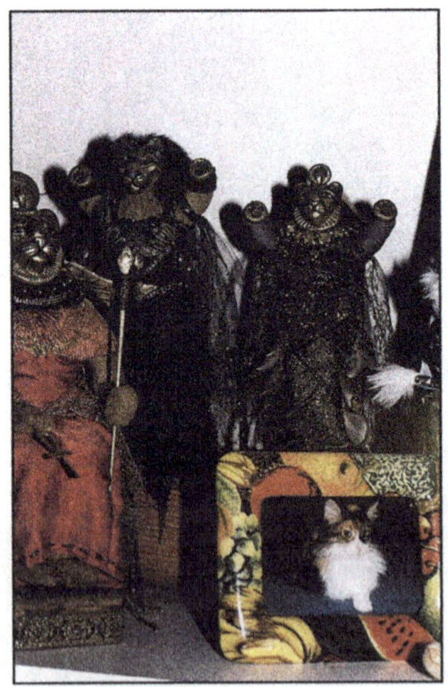

Plate 3. Karen Tate's altar, detail: cat figures by Catherine Farah. Left to right: Sekhmet (seated), Felina, and small standing Bast.

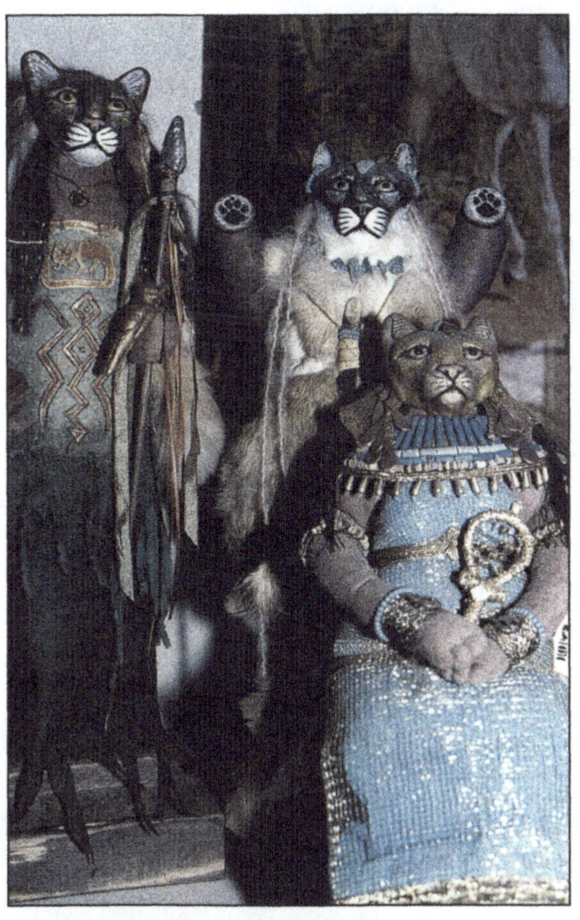

Plate 4. Karen Tate's altar, detail: cat figures by Catherine Farah. Left to right: Strength, Cougar, Bast (seated).

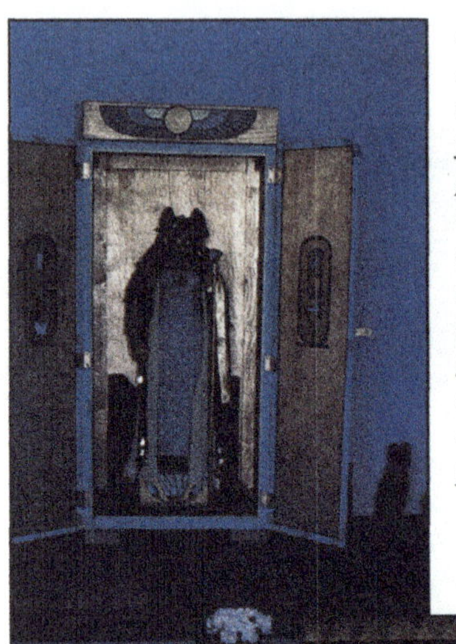

Plate 5. Bast shrine, by Catherine Farah. Located inside a converted shed in the artist's backyard, the triptych was made of plywood, then gilded and decorated with the goddess's sacred cartouches. The winged sun disk, symbol of the god Horus, is overhead. Inside the statue of the goddess Bast stands on a pedestal decorated with a lotus blossom, a symbol of Upper Egypt and a popular offering in ancient times.

Plate 6. Bast statue, by Catherine Farah; detail. This three-and-a-half-foot-tall statue is the largest Catherine has ever made. Otherwise, it resembles the artist's other statues in style and construction. All clothing and beadwork are handmade, and the statue's cape, scepter, and headdress are removable.

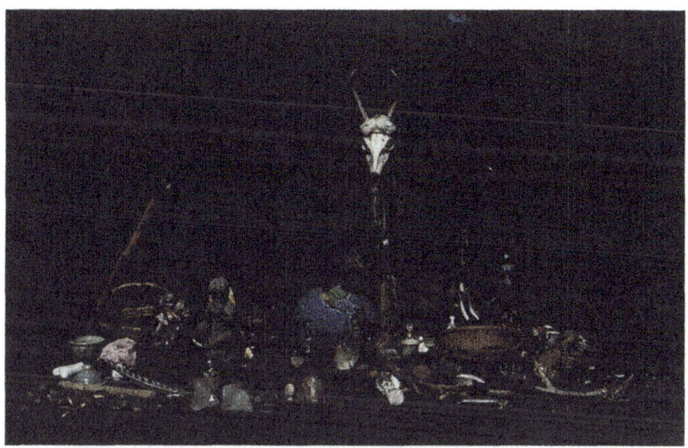

Plate 7. Communal altar, Pagan Spirit Gathering, Wisconsin, June 1993. The goat skull represents the horned god of death and rebirth. Note also the statuette of Pan, the Greek deity of woods and wild places; the globe, representing Mother Earth; and Barbie dressed as a Witch standing behind an altar. Pagan art typically incorporates many elements from popular culture.

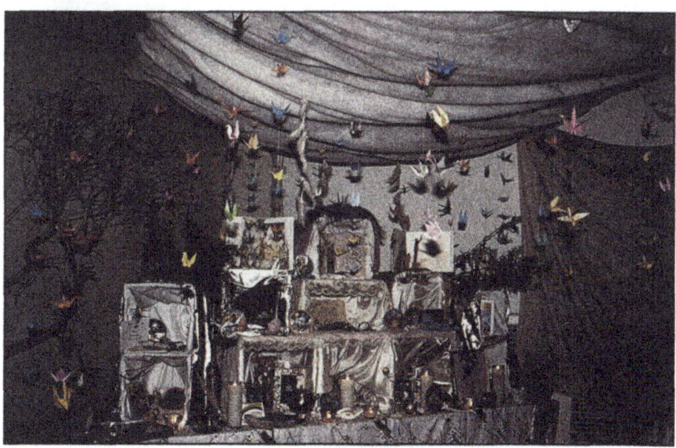

Plate 8. Air altar, Spiral Dance, San Francisco, October 1995. Fans hidden behind the drapery made the many paper cranes flutter continually in this evocative altar.

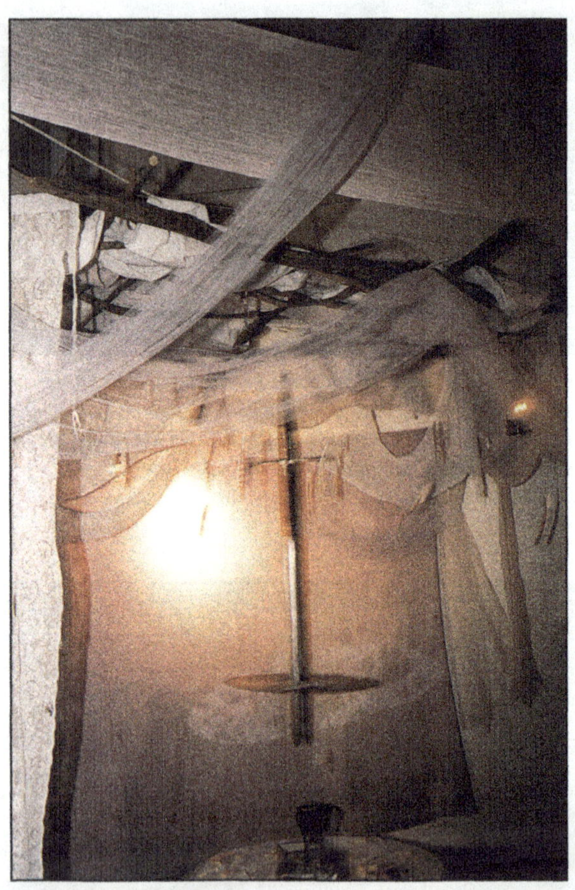

Plate 9. Air altar, Spiral Dance, San Francisco, October 1997. This is an air altar with a different meaning. Here, the sword suspended within the circular saw blade suggests the various uses to which blades can be put, including the destruction of living things.

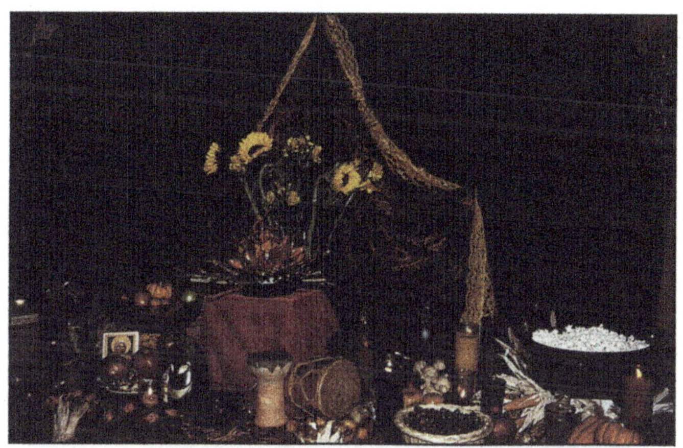

Plate 10. Fire altar, Spiral Dance, San Francisco, October 1995. The altar includes many red foods, hot foods, or foods that must be heated in order to become edible, such as popcorn.

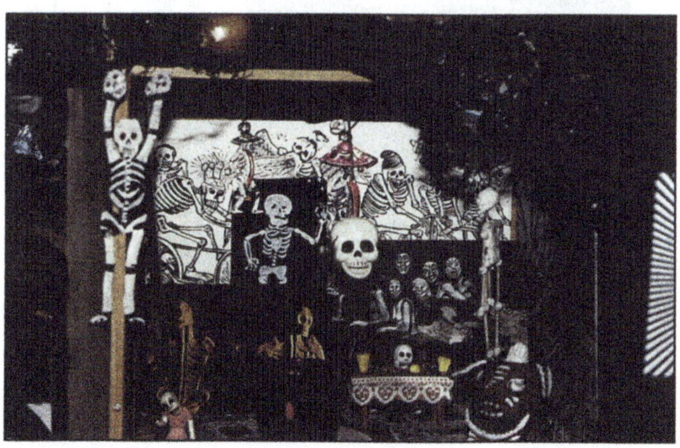

Plate 11. Earth altar, detail, Spiral Dance, San Francisco, October 1995. Skeleton motifs borrowed from Halloween and from El Día de los Muertos *adorn this vignette, which suggests that all living things return to the earth in death.*

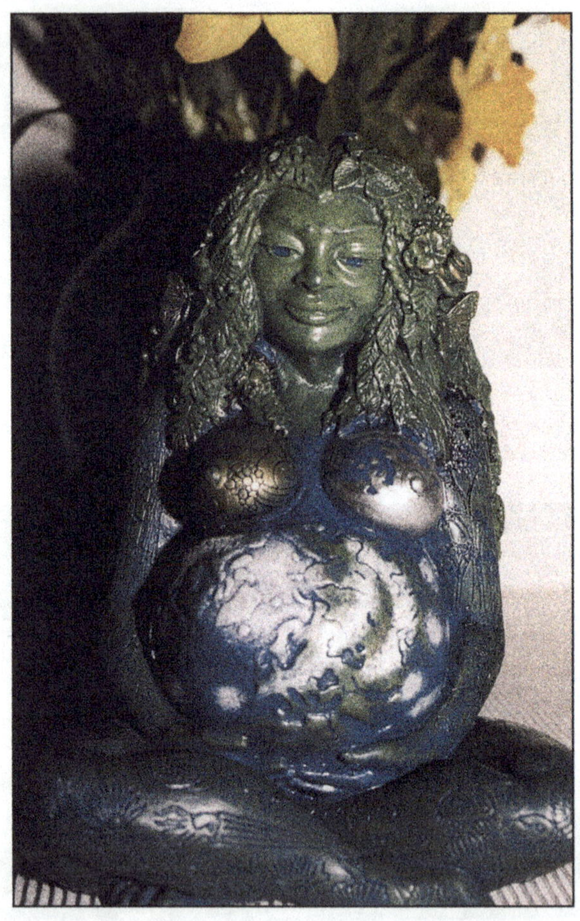

Plate 12. The Millennial Gaia, polyresin and acrylic, by Oberon Zell. From the collection of Arios and Jana of coven Ul.

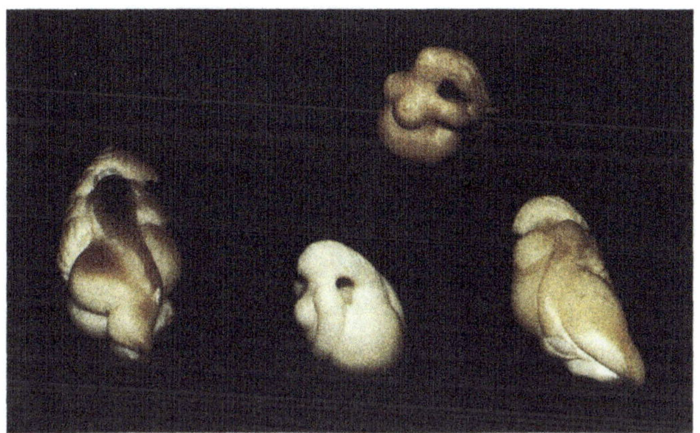

Plate 13. *Earth mother figurines, fossil tooth, by Reva Myers. In their form, they recall Neolithic female figurines, yet they also appear more streamlined and fluid. This aspect of the goddess is often associated with the full moon, fertility, creativity, nurturing, and protection.*

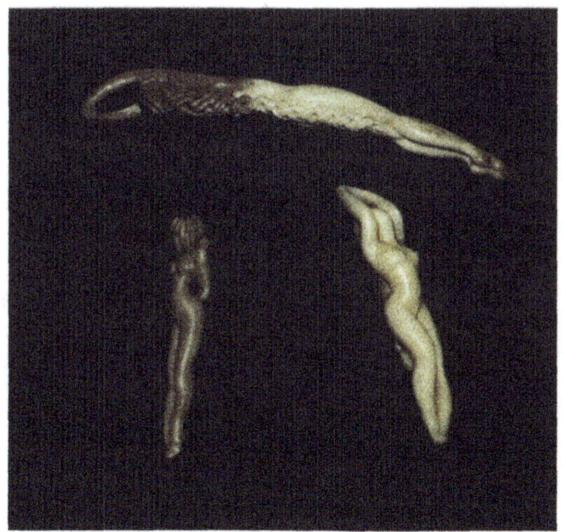

Plate 14. *Maiden goddess figurines, or "Pretty Ladies," antler, by Reva Myers. The goddess in her maiden form is often associated with the new moon, inspiration, and beginnings.*

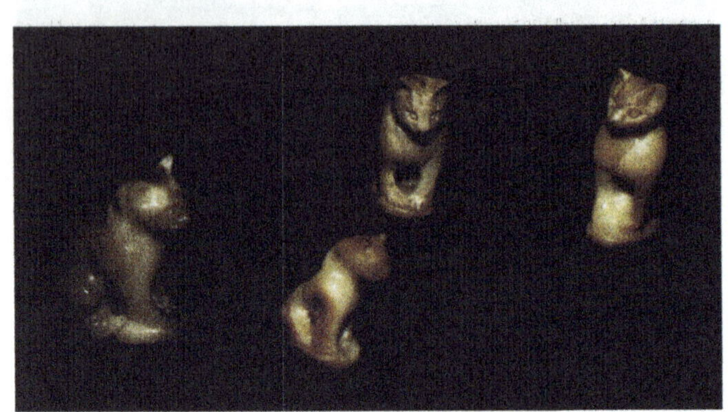

Plate 15. Cat figurines, carved fossil tooth, by Reva Myers.

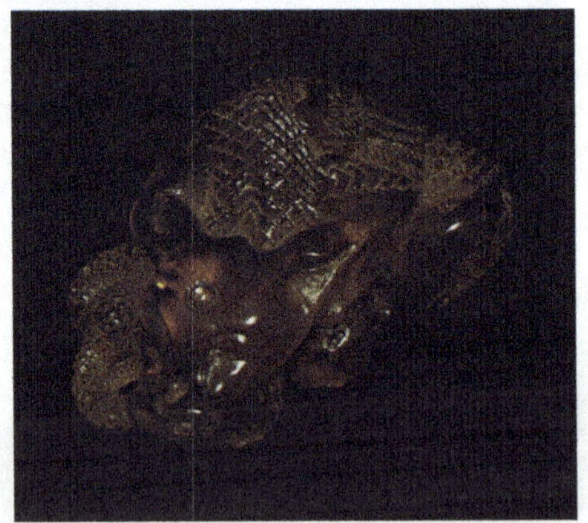

Plate 16. "Dragon Pup," carved amber, by Reva Myers.

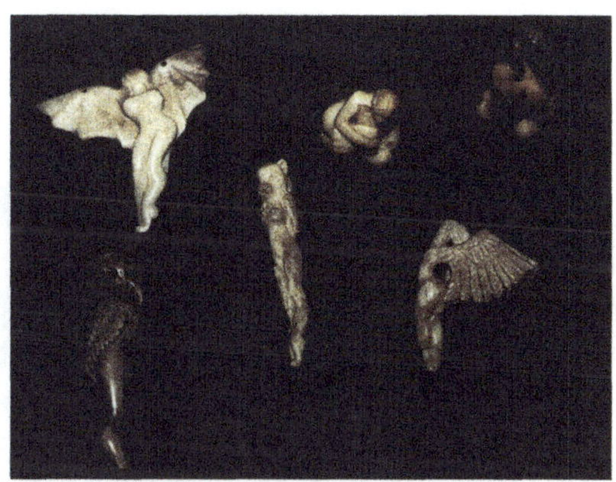

Plate 17. Animal-women, carved antler and fossil tooth, by Reva Myers.

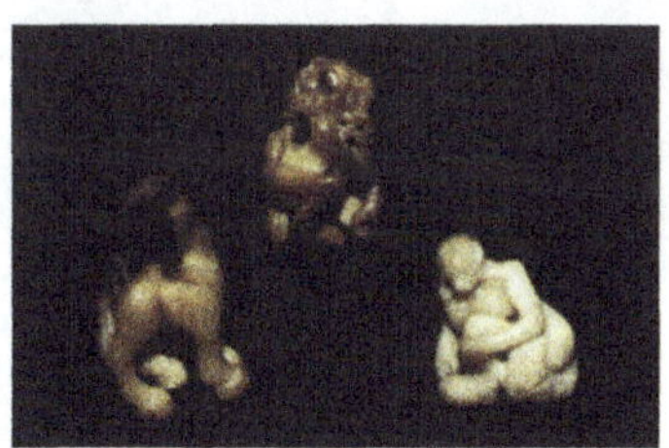

Plate 18. "Centaur-Woman,"
"Lion-Woman," and "Wolf-Girl,"
carved fossil tooth, by Reva Myers.

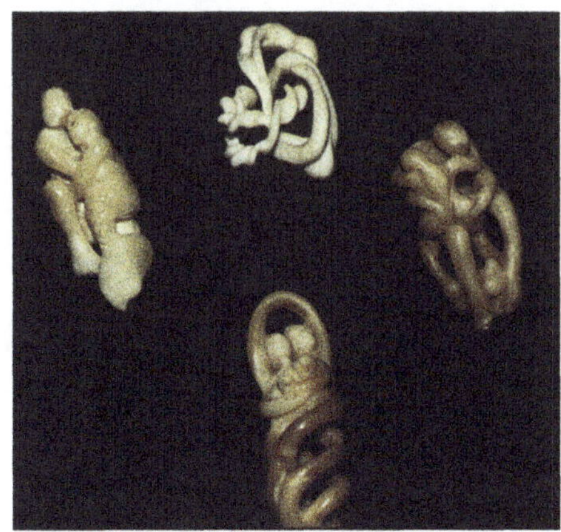

Plate 19. Intertwined male and female figures, carved antler and fossil tooth, by Reva Myers.

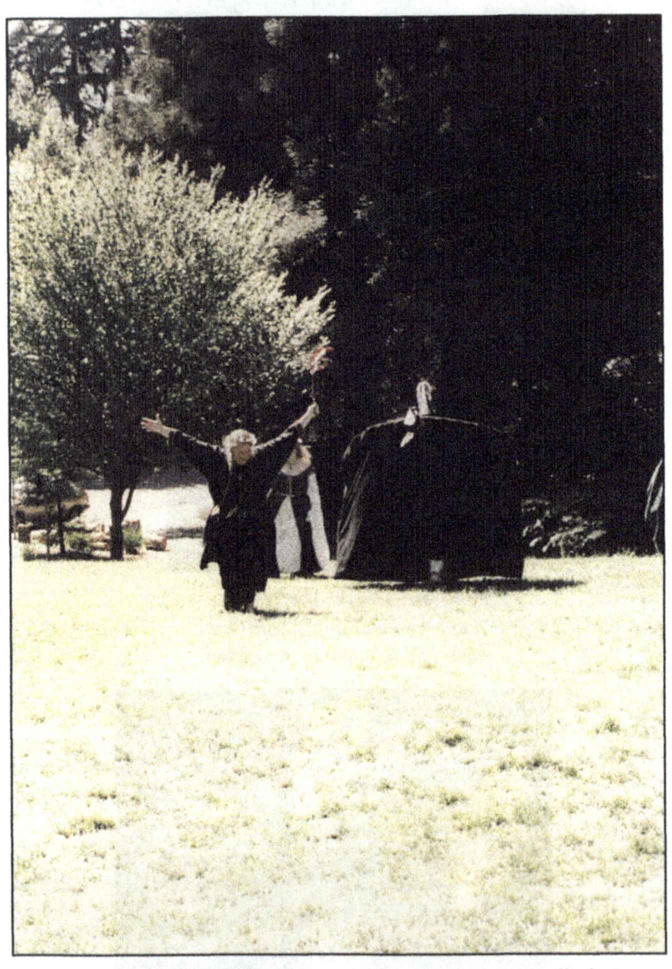

Plate 20. "'Oss 'oss!" "Wee 'oss!" Laurel Olson, as the teaser, calls the 'oss (D. H. Frew) into the circle at NROOGD's Beltaine ritual, Berkeley, May 1997.

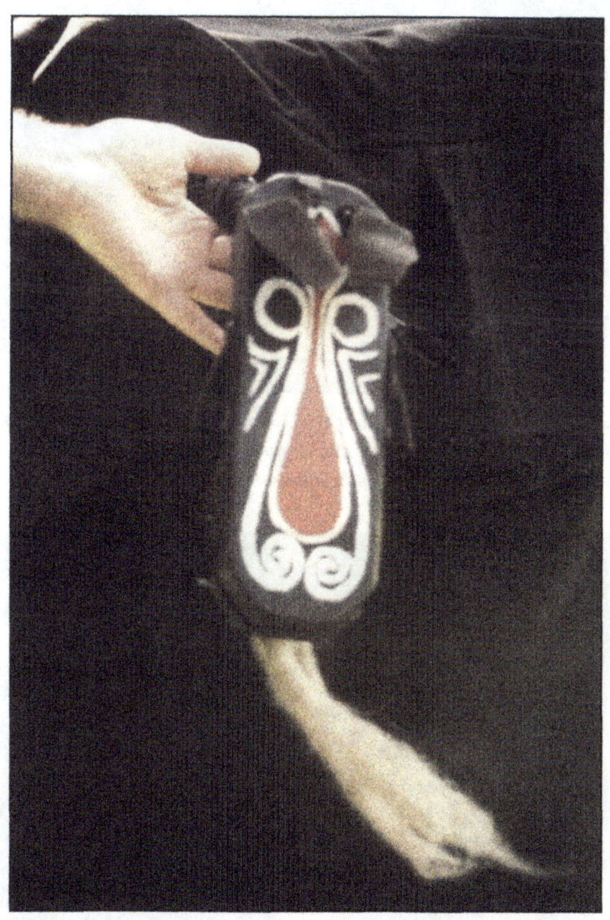

Plate 21. 'Oss's head with "snappers," detail, by Leigh Ann Hussey.

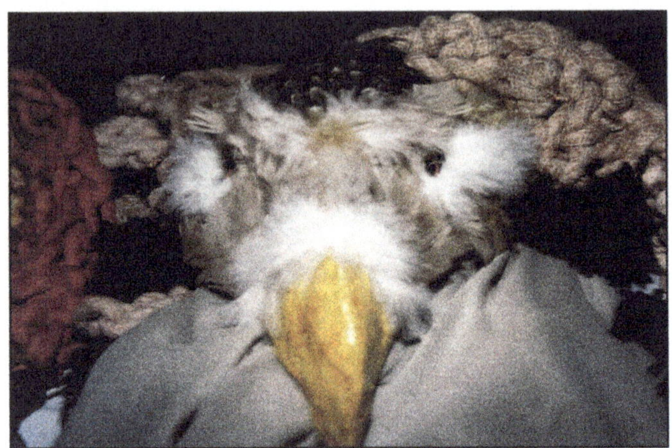

Plate 22. Bird mask, Merry Meet 1998, by Jana and coven Ul. The bird is associated with the element air and its qualities of intellectual curiosity, mental acuity, discernment, and communication.

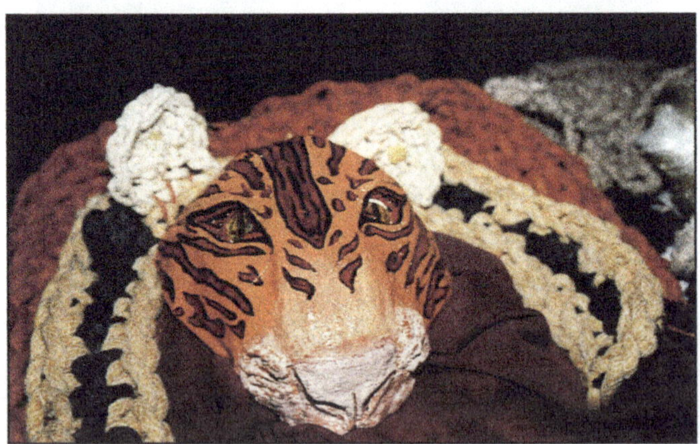

Plate 23. Fire cat mask, Merry Meet 1998, by Jana and coven Ul. Rather than being a specific kind of feline, the fire cat is designed to represent an ur-cat. Fire is associated with heat, strength, courage, passion, and will.

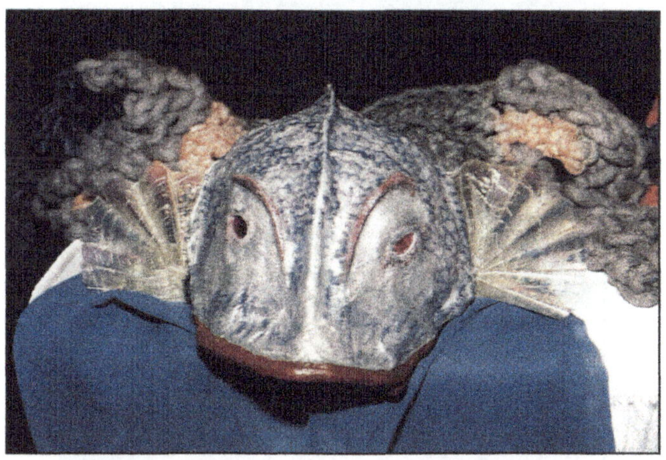

Plate 24. Fish mask, Merry Meet 1998, by Jana and coven Ul. The fish is associated with the element water and with intuition, imagination, daring, dreams, and the otherworld.

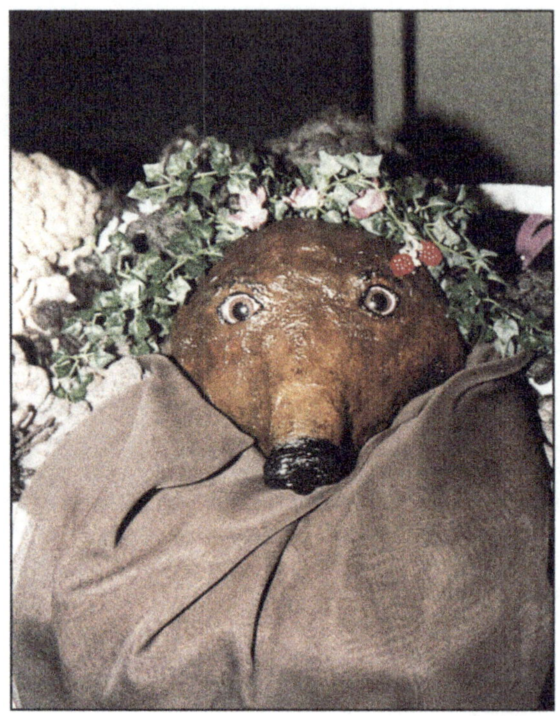

Plate 25. Bear mask, Merry Meet 1998, by Jana and coven Ul. The bear is associated with the element earth and its qualities of stability, permanence, nurturing, and fertility.

CPSIA information can be obtained at www.ICGtesting.com
Printed in the USA
BVOW11s0004300514

354906BV00004B/20/P